As Taught By My Father

Susan P. Protzman

Illustrated by Georgene Funk

Xulon Press

Xulon Press
2301 Lucien Way #415
Maitland, FL 32751
407.339.4217
www.xulonpress.com

Ilustrated by Georgene Funk
Cover painting by Georgene Funk

Unless otherwise indicated, Scripture quotations taken from the Holy Bible, New International Version (NIV). Copyright © 1973, 1978, 1984, 2011 by Biblica, Inc.™. Used by permission. All rights reserved.

Scripture quotations taken from the New American Standard Bible (NASB). Copyright © 1960, 1962, 1963, 1968, 1971, 1972, 1973, 1975, 1977, 1995 by The Lockman Foundation. Used by permission. All rights reserved.

Scripture quotations taken from The Holy Bible, Berean Study Bible (BSB). Copyright ©2016, 2018 by Bible Hub. Used by Permission. All Rights Reserved Worldwide.

Scripture quotations taken from the Holy Bible, New Living Translation (NLT). Copyright ©1996, 2004, 2007 by Tyndale House Foundation. Used by permission of Tyndale House Publishers, Inc.

Scripture quotations taken from the New King James Version (NKJV). Copyright © 1982 by Thomas Nelson, Inc. Used by permission. All rights reserved.

Scripture quotations taken from the King James Version (KJV) – public domain.

Printed in the United States of America.

ISBN-13: 978-1-6322-1720-2

Grasping our Father's Hand gives us confidence to trust and obey, as He leads us into our destiny. Together, we can fearlessly travel far beyond our expectations on the most incredible journey!

TABLE OF CONTENTS

INTRODUCTION

When we think about our legacy, it is hard for some of us to believe we even have one. We try to think of some grand thing we've done that would be marked as important. Stored in our memories are our stories; stories that have shaped our life. If our stories aren't told, they are lost forever—a lost treasure. For within those stories are God-given life lessons. He desires for us to come into a deeper relationship with Him. As we listen to His voice, God will reveal spiritual insights into our everyday experiences, that we've not understood before. Those stories and insights need to be shared and handed down to our descendants—generations of our children and grandchildren, so they can see how God worked in us and protected our spiritual heritage. Even now, I wish that I had written down more of the stories that my older relatives shared with me, but sadly, it's too late. Our legacy of faith, filled with our Father's wisdom, is the most valuable gift we can give our loved ones.

My first story began forming one morning as I was getting dressed to go to Bible study. The Lord began to speak to my heart about a humiliating encounter that caused me to feel irritated and miserable for days. His visit with me was far from being all 'sunshine and roses,' but it resolved the issue that was troubling me. Later at Bible study, while we were in our worship-prayer time, I felt compelled to share with them about my earlier encounter with God. After class, a friend told me that I should write that story down, so later in the evening, I did; I named it Humbled By Jello.

The next day at church, I gave a copy to my pastor, who read it and suggested that I submit it for publishing in the Upper Room devotional. The following morning as I prayed, I asked the Lord what I should do with the story. He told me that I was to put it in a book. I said, "What would I have to write about?" He said, "All the things that I have been teaching you and will be teaching you." Then I saw a picture of a book; on the front cover I saw His arm extending down from heaven, and my arm stretched up with my hand laying in His hand. The title was, As Taught By My Father, and I saw my name written on the bottom.

For me, this whole scenario started a month earlier, while I was reading about Abraham's willingness to obey God even if it meant sacrificing the life of his only son Isaac. God began stirring my heart, and then He nudged me to offer Him the things that I loved most in my life. So, I placed on the altar my love of reading books, teaching piano, camping, and being on the praise team. Through heartfelt tears, I surrendered them one by one, expecting God to receive them at that very moment as my sacrifice...but He sent no flame to consume them, and allowed them to remain there—at least for a time.

About two weeks later, while in prayer, the Lord told me that He was accepting my sacrificial offering—my love of reading books. In the emptiness of that space, I was to put a time of reading and studying the Bible every day. Only a few weeks later, God gave me a vision for this book, with the intention of transforming me from a reader to a writer. I felt unqualified for the assignment, yet my Father saw my life through a different perspective, the perspective of His Heavenly Kingdom.

He called my heart into a stance of 'obedience'. That may seem scary to you, or it might make you feel apprehensive, but in heaven's perspective, that obedience opens the door to a spiritual dimension known only by God. There may be plans for your destiny that the Lord has not revealed to you yet; a direction that may seem contrary to what you thought would be possible for your life. Don't underestimate the mind of God, nor His ability to work through you in impossible ways. It happened to me—most of who I thought I was, was not who my Father declared me to be.

Is there a longing in your soul to understand God's declaration over you? While you read about what my Father taught me in my stories, ask Him to help you apply those truths in your own story. Meditate on the Scripture passages and savor the words of God's Heart for you. I pray that you will be blessed as our heavenly Father guides you through the pages ahead. May He weave His thread of love, grace and wisdom into your life, not only affecting you, but touching your generations to come. May God be glorified as you personally engage in an incredible journey with Him.

ACKNOWLEDGEMENTS

Great is the Lord and most worthy of praise
his greatness no one can fathom.
One generation commends your works to another;
they tell of your mighty acts. Psalm 145:3-4

God is so worthy to be praised. Thank you, Father, for your faithfulness in my life. Thank you for your Holy Spirit, who stirred up my memories, thoughts, and intertwined them with your Word to bring forth stories that may bring hope and encouragement to many people.

I praise God for the rich heritage of my parents, Elsie and Harry Dodds, and my grandparents, who loved God and faithfully prayed throughout the generations of my family. I'm grateful that my Father preserved our lives so that we could serve Him and testify first-hand of His amazing grace.

God has truly blessed me with a wonderful husband, Dennis, who has lovingly supported me through the long process of writing this book. He has been my faithful partner and has encouraged me when I thought it would be much easier to give up. He always reminded me that this book was God's plan and that I needed to keep working on it until it was finished.

I'm very grateful for all my family, especially my adult children; Jennifer, Jeremy, Mark, and Todd, who, along with my grandchildren; Samantha, Sierra, Madison, Macayla, Jacob, Halei, and Noah were often great resources of inspiration. I really appreciate their kindness in allowing me to share some clips of their personal lives within my stories.

God has also blessed me with insightful mentors, Joanne Bennett and Ann Patterson. Together, we have sought the Lord many times when I needed God's direction. Over the years, they have been trusted sources, of Godly wisdom, concerning many spiritual matters. Once, when I had quit writing for a long time, Joanne walked over to me at Bible study, and then she gave me 'that look'—the stern, motherly one. Next, she handed me a pen and simply said, "The Lord said for you to get writing."

Before I knew about God's plan for this book, He had already pre-arranged everything that was needed, including an amazing editor. My mentor and great friend, Ann, just happened to be a former teacher, who minored in English. Most of her friends know she's a 'word person' who has always been a little obsessed with proper grammar. I'm so grateful for that fact, and for Ann, who has been like a special gift from heaven. She has blessed this book with countless hours of work, scrupulously editing every detail, and she has made sure that the Word of God was applied in a clear, precise manner.

Another dear friend, Georgene Funk, has been such a blessing. She's a tremendously gifted artist, whose detailed work leaves me in awe of her God-given talent. I'm grateful for all of her beautiful illustrations, which have truly enhanced this book with an endearing, whimsical look that brings a warm smile to our hearts, and life to the stories.

Also, I want to thank the Lord for my precious Tuesday Bible study ladies who have prayed for me, especially when I was struggling to complete this project. They literally prayed over the printed manuscript before it was sent to the publisher. The prayer of our hearts was that God would use this book in a mighty way to touch and encourage each person who reads it. We prayed they would be drawn into a deeper relationship with our Father.

May our Father be given the honor and glory that He deserves and may His Kingdom be multiplied. Thank you, Lord Jesus! Amen

Humbled by Jello

E arly this morning while I was getting ready to go to Bible study, the Lord began to deal with a situation that was troubling me. A few days ago, our family had gone to a wonderful, festive fall picnic. It was sunny, but a cool breeze kept the temperature perfect outside. Later that evening when it was time to pack up and go home, I went to the food table to gather my containers. Another lady, who was doing the same thing, sweetly asked me if I would like some jello salad to take home with me. Since it happened to be my favorite, I eagerly said, "Yes, I would love a piece." So, I handed her a dessert plate.

There was more than half of the of jello salad left in her glass dish, and I noticed there was a very small triangle-shaped piece sticking out in the center. I watched as she cut that tiny piece and put it on my plate. Then she used the spoon and scooped up all the pieces of fruit that other people had left behind. She scraped off the tidbits of jello still sticking around the edges of her dish. Then she proceeded to dump that on my little plate to fill it and to clean up her own container.

When I saw what she was doing, I thought, "Well, she's giving me everyone's leftover SLOP. When I get home, I'm dumping THAT into the garbage!" I felt very insulted that she didn't just give me one full portion of the fruited jello salad with the yummy topping. Although I kindly thanked her, she had no idea how this really made me feel. I went home holding onto my dessert plate of indignation, but for some reason I couldn't dump it into the garbage, so I put it in the refrigerator on the shelf.

For days, every time I opened the door, I could see that dish sitting there. Bumping into it again this morning, I thought, "I will never ever offer leftovers to anyone unless I give them the best portion." Then, as God was speaking to my heart, I thought about times when there had been food drives. Had I gone to our shelves and gathered cereal, canned fruit, vegetables, and box mixes that my family didn't seem to like? Was I actually just getting rid of unwanted excess which had been left there for months? Or had I looked at our food and selected the items that were our favorites, hoping to bless those families. The Lord was showing me that I needed to offer my very best portion.

God's stirring continued and I began to think about the times that we do the same thing with God. Some days we are so busy that we may only take a few minutes to sit quietly, pray, and read the Bible before we're off and running. Throughout the day, we may spoon and scoop up a prayer need that was left behind. Or we may scrape off some tidbits of praise for Him. It's like that plate of jello salad...it has a small piece intact with a lot of leftover SLOP dumped around it.

But then the Lord went one step further, and I knew that I needed to change the WE word to ME, for I could see myself handing Him that same plate of indignation. And I could see Him reluctantly putting it in the refrigerator on the shelf, looking at it occasionally... wishing that He too had been offered a full portion of my very best.

LET'S TALK ~ GOD'S HEART FOR YOU

Although I wrote "Humbled by Jello" a few years ago, to this day I cannot read the last line without a few tears. It broke my heart to realize that I had been offering the Lord a "plate of indignation" so often throughout my life. When I asked God to show me what a full portion would be, he led me to an Old Testament passage which told about the Feast of the First Fruits.

Leviticus 23:9-10 (NAS) Then the LORD spoke to Moses, saying, "Speak to the sons of Israel and say to them, 'When you enter the land which I am going to give to you and reap its harvest, then you shall bring in the sheaf (a bundle) of the first fruits of your harvest to the priest.'"

This feast required that a tithe of the first crop, which each family harvested, would be offered to God. The Israelites were commanded to not eat the food from their harvest until they had made this offering. That's how important it was to God. It was a matter of the heart for them to offer Him the best possible portion, the ripest, the freshest, and the most succulent produce of the harvest. God didn't need the food, of course. He wanted to instill an attitude of gratitude deep in their spirit. It was vital for them to always trust, praise, and honor God as Jehovah Jireh, the One who provided for them.

Today, God is still our provider. And He still expects us to set aside His portion first, not last. Giving leftovers to God is no way to express thanks. Clearly, by the end of this jello story, I knew the Lord was leading me to look at more than my financial tithing and willingness to generously share with others. I knew He wanted me to evaluate the offering of my time with Him. I knew God was more concerned with, and specifically targeting, my lack of discipline with it. He was asking me for the first hours in my morning and for it to be a tithing of the hours in my day. A few hours seemed like a huge commitment. How would it be possible to fit that into my schedule! But God, in His wisdom, knew how much time would be necessary for Him to prepare me for new ministry opportunities in my life...all of which have required my complete reliance on Him.

I pray that the Holy Spirit may be stirring up your heart right now to seriously take the challenge to reassess some areas of your life. Ask the Lord to show you where you may not be offering Him your best, full portion. Don't hesitate or be afraid of feeling vulnerable before God. It's not too painful compared to picturing God's refrigerator shelf filled with the plates of SLOP which you may be giving Him.

Psalm 26:2 (NAS) says, "Examine me, O Lord, and try me; test my mind and my heart."

Seek God and align yourself with His heart. Our Father is loving and merciful. His corrective words are more encouraging than painful. He may be waiting for you to come to this very moment of openness and commitment to receive a new mandate for your life. Don't miss out on anything that God has set forth for you. Don't wait to be humbled by jello. What unexpected, wondrous opportunities has God prepared for you? Aren't you, at least, curious?

Reflection: Lord, purify my heart and lead me into Your greater purpose for my life.

Meditation music: Give Us Clean Hands (Christian contemporary-available on internet) or Have Thine Own Way, Lord (Traditional hymn)

Humble Jello
(originally Apricot Salad)

1 can apricots & 1 can crushed pineapple (drain for an hour-save juice)

(dissolve and chill) 3 small boxes orange jello

4 ½ cup boiling water

1 cup of the saved juice mixture

When chilled, fold in ¾ cup mini marshmallows & drained fruit

Pour into a 9x13 container & refrigerate

Topping: In a small saucepan, mix together:

½ cup sugar

1Tablespoon flour

1 egg

1 cup saved juice mixture

Cook until thickened, stirring constantly

Then add and stir in: 2 Tablespoons butter

Set aside to cool to room temperature. Meanwhile prepare:

Whip 1 cup of whipping cream and sweeten (or use 8 oz. cool whip)

Mix whipped topping with cooled, cooked mixture & spread over jello.

Top with ¾ cup shredded cheddar cheese. Refrigerate

2.

Bees in my Bonnet

When I think about some of the special times in my childhood, I can remember myself when I was about five years old. That summer, my mom had my long curls cut off for a cooler, little pixie hairstyle. I spent most of my playtime wearing my cowgirl hat with a cowgirl holster buckled around my hips. My older brother was my best friend, and we were always playing together. We loved to pretend that we lived in the old west. Back in those days, westerns were the most popular type of action-adventure television show, at least in our house.

Some days we would argue about who would get to be the sheriff with the badge, and who had to be the robber with a handkerchief tied around their face to hold up the stagecoach. Other days, when there were more kids around, we would play cowboys and Indians.

There was one day that I can remember as clearly as if it happened yesterday. I was playing outside alone near the porch steps of our house, when I began to hear the beating of drums. As the beat continued, I kept looking around trying to figure out where it was coming from, and wondering when it would stop. Steadily, the drums played on and on, and it dawned on me that it had to be coming from the woods. It had to be the sound of Indians on the warpath!

Instead of running into the house to safety or telling my parents, I sat down on the steps, spellbound. I couldn't take my eyes off of the woods. I just knew that at any moment I would see Indians, with scary painted faces, coming out from behind all those trees. I knew we were going to be attacked by flaming arrows. Already the fear of the unknown, and of the impending doom, had paralyzed me. It held me defenseless and completely captive...

Not long ago, I opened my Bible to Psalm 115. Before I read it, I glanced at the study notes which said Psalms115-118 were traditionally sung at the Passover meal, celebrating Israel's escape from slavery in Egypt. I was reminded that they certainly knew how it felt to be defenseless and completely captive for hundreds of years! So, I decided to read the entire passage, instead of just one chapter. When I came to Psalm 118:10-14, the Lord started nudging me to pay close attention. It said:

> "All the nations surrounded me,
> but in the name of the Lord I cut them off.
> They surrounded me on every side,
> but in the name of the Lord I cut them off.
> They swarmed around me like bees,
> but they died out as quickly as burning thorns;
> in the name of the Lord I cut them off.
> I was pushed back and about to fall,
> but the Lord helped me.
> The Lord is my strength and my song;
> he has become my salvation."

Wondering what the Lord was trying to show me, I read it again. I realized that God wanted me to understand that the *nations that surrounded me* were those big things in my life that hover over me like a towering enemy, ready and waiting to attack: things like financial problems, stress, health problems, unforgiveness, rebellious children, and things that Satan can use to consume my attention and distract me from God. Most of those big things seemed to be in order so I moved on.

The passage read, "They swarmed around me like bees, but they died out as quickly as burning thorns; in the name of the Lord I cut them off." The Lord pointed out that those swarming bees are like the annoying things that happen in my day that try to affect my peace and joy, such as telemarketers, arguing children, a rain soggy newspaper, mistakes on my grocery receipt, and the list could go on. They are just little bees in my bonnet, that if not swatted down when they first appear can accumulate like that swarm. The scripture states that "they (the bees) died out as quickly as burning thorns; in the name of the Lord, I cut them off." God was showing me that I need to take action as soon as it begins to happen. I need to speak out loud with authority, "In the name of the Lord I cut them off." Declare it to be so!

After seeing all the things that the Lord was showing me, I closed the Bible and went about my day. I kept thinking about *the nations that surround*. I had been convinced that I didn't have anything big looming over me, but I said "Lord, if I have any nation in my life, show me." Immediately, God spoke, "Your new campers are a nation in your life." I gasped and was startled because I wasn't expecting to get such a quick response. When I thought about it, God was right, of course!

For many years, we have had our camper at a campground parked on a hillside, in a wooded area, with only a few other campers nearby. There has never been anyone along the whole left side of our camping area, and it has been such a quiet, peaceful retreat for us. One weekend when we went to camp, the owners had moved not just one camper, but three campers onto that empty space beside us. I was so upset all weekend that I couldn't stand to look over in that direction. I moped around and wallowed in self-pity, truly grieving for my loss of privacy. I was so caught up in emotional distress, I had completely ignored God all weekend.

The Lord showed me that this issue was indeed a nation hovering. I needed to cut off the effects of it, so "In the name of the Lord I cut it off." I asked God to forgive me. Then I saw a picture of myself with both hands outstretched, carrying pies to those families, who unknowingly were part of my problem. I knew that I had to obediently follow through and make amends, even though they didn't have a clue about Who was motivating my peace offering. That was between God and me.

Sometimes we are like that little child playing by the porch steps, spellbound by fear and paralyzed by impending doom. We may not even see the enemy or recognize what is drawing us away from God. We need to ask God to show us. If there is sin in our life, stress, or unresolved issues, they can buzz around us like swarming bees. They can oppressively cast a shadow over us, just like an enemy nation. They can loom and hover, if not dealt with, and can hold us defenseless and completely captive. Psalm 118:13-14 tells us that when we are about to fall, the Lord will help us. He is our strength and song; He is our salvation. When we need rescued, we should never hesitate to call on the powerful, mighty name of Jesus. It's our privilege as His children; we belong to Him.

By the way, I didn't need to be rescued by the Lord when I was facing an Indian attack at age five. Later, I found out that the drums I heard that day were from my neighbor Sally's record. The music was soft, so she had turned it up louder to hear it while she worked outside. As she opened more of her windows, the drums that were loud became louder. But strangely, only the sound of the drum beat echoed up to my house.

When I shared my story, and what God was teaching me, with some friends, I was told that I needed to include verse 15. They were absolutely right. Psalm 118:15 declares that, "Shouts of joy and victory resound in the tents of the righteous; The Lord's right hand has done mighty things!" My first exposed nation began because of my attitude at camp. But the Lord's mighty hand restored my joy, and His victory song filled my heart!

LET'S TALK ~ GOD'S HEART FOR YOU

Have you ever felt spellbound by fear or circumstances that were hovering over your life? Do you sometimes feel like something is opposing and holding you down from getting out of a mundane rut you seem to be in? Maybe you are feeling clueless about how to escape out of that pit.

I remember times in my life when there was nothing more that I could do to turn around a situation. My only option was to surrender it to God. Often the turmoil was the result of bad choices, sometimes mine; other times it was someone else in my family whose actions affected all of us. I've had critical seasons of grieving the unexpected loss of a loved one that threw me into a pit of oppression. Those traumatic times can be paralyzing, and it can be nearly impossible to pull yourself out of the depths of sadness. Then, only God can tug us out of our troubled crisis and rescue us from falling in deeper.

Psalm 40:1-3a "I waited patiently for the Lord; he turned to me and heard my cry. He lifted me out of the slimy pit, out of the mud and mire; he set my feet on a rock and gave me a firm place to stand. He put a new song in my mouth, a hymn of praise to our God."

Psalm 103:4 "(God) redeems your life from the pit and crowns you with love and compassion." When God lifts us out of that slimy pit, He sets our feet on solid ground and crowns us with His love and compassion. Only our Heavenly Father can touch us in such a way that His living water springs forth, bringing healing, comfort and renewal to our souls! Our weary heartache is soothed as the Lord begins to fill us with a new song and unexplainable joy.

Because of God's great love, He has given us amazing Scriptures that remind us of the powerful authority that we inherited as His children. I love Psalm 118:10-14, because it clearly tells us that we should not allow issues to pester us like swarming bees. We are not to be intimidated by them, because the powerful Holy Spirit lives in us. We carry the name of Jesus, and we need to speak it out loud to break the enemy's game plan to wear us down spiritually. Those bees carry out a sneaky, devilish attack on our sanity and sanctity. If nations are towering over us like giants, we need to immediately call out to God to conquer them. Otherwise, they may progress to an oppression which can be disabling.

God's Heart is to encourage and teach you to utilize the weapons of warfare that you already possess, in order to dismantle the enemy's plan against you. Never forget John 10:10 which tells us that the thief is out to kill, steal and destroy. The verse continues to declare that God's plans are to give you an abundant life. You can't be living abundantly if you are always on the defensive end of the spiritual sword. You need to be standing firm in the offensive stance, prepared for any evil shenanigans that the devil drums up to pester and wear you down.

Hebrew 4:12 says, "For the word of God is alive and active. Sharper than any double-edged sword, it penetrates even to dividing soul and spirit, joints and marrow; it judges the thoughts and attitudes of the heart." There's such power in knowing and speaking the Word of God. It's infallible against the enemy's onslaught of deception that tries to under-mine your peace and faith. Knowing God's Word brings freedom from depending on your own understanding, which can be detrimental to keeping you within God's boundaries of protection that surround you with His protection.

Proverbs 3:5-6 (NASB) encourages us to: "Trust in the LORD with all your heart and lean not on your own understanding. In all your ways acknowledge Him, and He will keep your paths straight." If your heart is not fully trusting in God, fear and wild imaginations will leave you sitting immobilized on the porch steps like an imma-ture child, staring wide-eyed into impending doom. That's living in abundant captivity. Abundant life is living boldly under the mercy of God who gives you confidence to face the unknown with insight and power. You are the righteousness of Christ; you carry His name. Together, you can face any situation.

No power from hell can cause you to forfeit the victorious life that Jesus has made possible for all who love Him. Grow up and mature into the spiritual, mighty warrior that you were created to be. Walk in such a way that brings honor and glory to your Father. Utilize every moment of your lifetime to accomplish your sacred destiny. Stay the course, keep your eyes on the goal set before you, stop just swatting the bees in your bonnet. Once and for all, cut them off in the name of the Lord for the Name of Jesus is powerful!

Reflection: Lord, show me every issue in my life that needs rectified by Your power.

Meditation music: Isn't the Name (contemporary) or There is Power in the Blood (hymn)

3.

Dandelions

A month ago, we had to dig up the front yard and replace some old drainage pipes. What a muddy mess, but the work had to be done. After a few weeks of letting the dirt settle, it was time to rake and shovel out the rocks, so the soil was ready to reseed. My adult son kiddingly said, "Too bad grass seed doesn't come with some weed seed mixed in, so it can match the rest of your yard!" It was pretty funny, because he was right. We have never been too worried about the weeds that have infiltrated our yard since it was originally planted.

I remember growing up in the house next door to where I live now. We always had grass with plenty of yellow blossoming dandelions growing among the green. I thought they were beautiful, just like little sunshine faces. I was really delighted that our flowers regrew so fast after we mowed. All of the neighborhood kids, who came to my home to hang out, enjoyed picking them. We spent hours making long chains, necklaces, and bracelets out of the hollow stems. Even when the flowers had died, we would pick them and wait for a breeze to come. Then we would raise our arms high in the air to shake them, until the fluffy seeds were blowin' in the wind. It was fascinating to see how far they would travel.

I thought we were so fortunate to have so many more yellow flowers than the neighbors had in their yards.

About a decade later, when I was grown up, I was surprised to find out that dandelions are considered weeds and that most people hate seeing them grow in their yards. As a matter of fact, I was told that some of the very same children I played with had been taught how to get rid of dandelions. Many times, they had watched their dad, with his bucket, using a tool to dig deep to get the roots of the weed. While he worked, they had used their little sand buckets and digger to try to help him. If the ground was too hard, they would clean up the yard by gathering acorns. To this day, many decades later, with all their children raised, this neighbor still has the most beautifully manicured lawn. In spite of the weed seeds that have randomly blown across the borderline driveway from our yard to theirs, they have been wonderful neighbors—full of grace toward our lack of lawn etiquette.

As I write this, I am wondering why God is leading me to these thoughts. Sometimes it takes a while to figure Him out. So, let's dig in the dirt for a little bit. About 15 years ago, God decided it was time to do some dramatic spiritual landscaping at my house. He took on quite a challenge in preparing my soil for the seeds He wanted to plant. He had to rake up lots of stones. Stones of self-doubt, fear, timidity, and especially stubbornness that kept me in a mindset of self-protection. God had to chop up old roots of lies that the enemy devil had grown to keep me contained. As He shoveled those twisted shoots into the wheel barrow to be burnt, amazing things began to change deep in my soul. God began showing me that my worth was to be found in Him alone. My value was priceless in His esteem. My confidence would be dependent on my dependence on Him each day.

God then began to open my heart to overflow with an unconditional love for the people He put in my life. My Father started teaching me to see them through His eyes. He filled me with His compassion to feel their hurts and pain. He gave me His words to speak over them to bring healing and hope.

During that time period when God was stirring that up in me, I had gone to a music store to buy tickets for a musical. A man, who was one of the actors, had set up a table in the corner to handle the sales. I noticed that he avoided eye contact with people and seemed a little timid and mousy. He was quietly withdrawn, rather distant. He looked a little sickly, and his disorderly hair was greasy. After I bought the tickets, I went back to my car, and the Lord showed me a glimpse of my hand laying on his messy hair, praying. I felt like my heart was melting with an overwhelming sense of compassion for him. So, I prayed immediately and continued to pray every time God brought him to my thoughts.

The next week after seeing the production, the Lord moved my heart to write a long letter to this actor. God had shown me two sides of this man. One personality struggled with very low self-worth and avoided interaction with people. The other side morphed from a caterpillar to a brilliant butterfly to receive man's applause. His soul longed for those few minutes of approval. He was one of the supporting actors, who had a few lines in many of the scenes. God had me share with him that every time he came on stage, all eyes followed him because of his great talent. I told him that he skillfully and flamboyantly stole the audience's heart and drew all the attention away from the main characters!

Then the Lord wanted me to make it clear to the actor that he was blessed with that extra special gift of talent from God. His Heavenly Father created and loved him beyond any earthly relationship he had ever experienced in this life. There was a lot more that I was led to write, including the fact that God had me praying for him every day. After the actor read the letter, with tear-filled eyes he told my husband, who was the set carpenter, that no one had ever said those words that I had written in the letter. It meant so much to him, and he was sincerely grateful. God had touched his heart in a powerful way. Maybe he had never understood God's heart for him.

So, what's the connection between this actor and my dandelions? As I was writing this morning, I looked up information about dandelions. Although they are considered weeds to many people, that is not what God created them to be. Surprisingly, they are not even native to this country. Dandelions originated in Europe and Asia and were highly valued. They were a dependable, common food source, since everything from the root to the flower head is edible. Historians believe that dandelions were brought to America on ships by the early colonists on purpose, because of their nutritional and medicinal value. I remember my husband's grandparents used to pick the early, tender leaves for spring salad. Some people have made them into dandelion wine. But I have never heard anyone talk about the healing potential of this plant.

Evidently, most people are unaware of the dandelion's flamboyant versatility which God ordained for this misunderstood, underestimated plant. The world often despises what God has created to fulfill His plan and purpose on this earth. People's perception, often formed by deception, reveals the craftiness of Satan. He is always behind, twisting truth into lies. And he thrives at demeaning and destroying what God has made to be excellent and praiseworthy.

The life of the dandelion represents so many of us, like the actor, who have been mislabeled and victimized by the enemy. He has often convinced us that we are worthless, and we begin to withdraw emotionally from life and the people around us. We try to avoid more hurt, which can cause our spirits to become dulled from the painfulness of it all. The devil hates that God created us in His own image. He hates that we are each given special abilities to touch the lives of others for the sake of Christ. God made us to live a life worthy of our calling, so our life would display His glory. That's why the enemy watches for every opportunity to discredit the good and perfect plan of our Heavenly Father.

God blessed me with a simple, child-like heart, so that I would always love the beautiful yellow dandelions of this world. He designed my yard—my life—to flourish with those lovely sunshine faces of unique, talented friends and acquaintances who humbly undermine their own amazing abilities and value. God gave me a deep sense of love and compassion to treasure and encourage each one He plants within my borders. They are mightily ordained by God, and some have been a true source of Godly insight, who have brought wisdom and healing into my life. They continually delight me.

But even more so, God is delighted when dandelions become undaunted and display their beautiful blooms, thriving and growing bravely, tall above the grass. They have become fearless of being mowed down, confident of God's restoring power to revive them again and again.

Probably in a few weeks, my husband will rake the straw off of the newly seeded lawn. I expect it to resemble the neighbor's perfectly manicured, lush yard. I'm not holding on to any hope of seeing dandelions. But if in time, little yellow sunshine faces mysteriously begin to pop up, the only clue I will give my husband will be, "the answer my friend, is blowin' in the wind, the answer is blowin' in the wind…"

LET'S TALK ~ GOD'S HEART FOR YOU

Truly, the answer to life's questions will never be found in silly phrases of a song, like 'blowin in the wind.' It's only in the wind of God's Spirit that insight is given to our questions. We are such a product of our past and our childhood. Good, bad, or sometimes silly—our thoughts recall them. Growing up in the 1950-60s, our home was filled with Southern Gospel and Folk music, which accounts for my love for Jesus and my childlike perception of life. I remember singing a lot of songs from our Peter, Paul, and Mary album, like 'Puff the Magic Dragon' and 'Blowin' in the Wind.' Although I knew every word, the true meaning of this music escaped my innocence. Who knew many of the folk songs were about worldly social injustice! Certainly not me. I was a happy, carefree kid, who played outside barefoot, climbed trees, and loved picking dandelions.

It's surprising how God can remind us of the past, then mingle it with the present to bring a deeper insight into our future. For each person, the scenario is vividly different, yet it is pointing to what we have in common. We are designed by God to fulfill the destiny that was chosen for us—a life that brings honor and joy to our Father, who has blessed us with mercy and grace.

Living a Life Worthy of our Calling: God's heart is that you would live your life worthy of the calling He placed on you. He desires that you would flourish, using the gifts and talents He has given you in a way that is directly connected to His purpose for your life. These special abilities reflect the greatness of God and

His salvation plan, which redeemed you for bearing good fruit, being successful, and serving Him.

In Colossians 1:9-11 the Apostle Paul writes "... We continually ask God to fill you with the knowledge of his will through all the wisdom and understanding that the Spirit gives, so that you may live a life worthy of the Lord and please him in every way: bearing fruit in every good work, growing in the knowledge of God, being strengthened with all power..." As you believe and speak this Word of Truth over your life, the Holy Spirit will give you knowledge, wisdom, understanding, and will strengthen you with power to overcome any enemy lies meant to derail you from God's ordained direction.

Spiritual Transformation: God's heart is that you would begin to see yourself as He sees you—pure and holy. Christ died to reconcile you to Himself—not only to save, but to declare that you are without blemish and free from derogatory accusations. Colossians 1:21-22 says "Once you were alienated from God... but now God has reconciled you by Christ's physical body through death to present you holy in His sight, without blemish and free from accusation."

Colossians 3:1-2 "Since then, you have been raised with Christ, set your hearts on things above, where Christ is seated at the right hand of God. Set your minds on things above, not on earthly things." You have been raised from death with Christ, who sits at the right hand of God. Picture yourself sitting in the heavenly throne room with only your feet dangling on this earth. Spiritual change comes when you begin to refocus to see yourself in light of your heavenly position with Christ.

Colossians 3:10 "...Put on the new self, which is being renewed in knowledge in the image of its Creator." Remember that you were created in God's image. He wants to continually transform your mind to be more like His, so you can discern His good, pleasing, and perfect will. The transforming of your mind, heart and soul by the Holy Spirit is the only way that emotional hurt and woundedness from the past can ever be fully healed. Pray and ask the Spirit to help you. Look up verses that speak truth and healing. Write them down and pray them over yourself. Declare them out loud so the enemy flees.

Our Worth and Confidence in God: The world wants you to believe that you are worthless, a loser, and unwanted, often treating you like an annoying weed. God's heart is that you would know that you are loved and treasured. Truthfully, you are more valuable than the dandelion that has amazing potential from its root to the blossom.

Luke 12:6 (NLT) tells us that "The very hairs on your head are all numbered...you are more valuable to God than a whole flock of sparrows." Believe that God cares about every tiny detail in your life. You are loved. Everything that has come against you in the past that has caused disillusionment, pain, discouragement, or self-loathing concerns Him. You have been victimized by Satan.

God's heart is that your life would not be derailed or destroyed by the enemy, but that you would live each day spiritually strengthened, renewed, and restored. You can be assured that you are highly favored of God and blessed. Jeremiah 17:7 tells us, "Blessed is the one who trusts in the Lord, whose confidence is in him." Fully place your trust and confidence in the Lord, and you will flamboyantly flourish to display the beauty of God. Nothing will be able to hinder you from fulfilling every good and perfect plan prepared for you. And forever, as long as your feet dangle on this earth, keep your dandelion face focused toward the heavenly light. With great anticipation, envision that the seeds of your life are blowin' in the wind of God's Spirit, and trust that they will be planted wherever He pleases!

Reflection: Am I walking boldly, with confidence in the Lord, knowing that I am dearly loved and treasured by my heavenly Father, who watches over me night and day?

Meditation music: You Say (Contemporary) or His Eye is on the Sparrow (Hymn)

4.

Singing in the Rain

There's a refreshing worship song with lyrics that make me long to experience the waterfall of God. It reminds me of intimate times I've spent with my Father, reading His Book. Each morning, I can almost hear Him calling my name to receive this outpouring of love. I run with anticipation to see His message written just for me. As the music continues, it stirs a wondrous desire in my soul to be drenched in His presence and to be washed clean from my imperfections and sin. After an interlude, the music begins to fade out and unexpectedly ends with: "I'm singing in the rain...what a wonderful feeling...I'm happy again."

The song reminded me of a day last spring, when I came out of a store and saw that it had started to sprinkle large raindrops. Right away a grumbling attitude surfaced from an ugly corner of my mind, and I became very irritated with what was inevitably going to happen. My brain began flashing photo clips of my moussed, hair-sprayed hair flattened into a matted, sticky clump. With a shopping cart stacked full of groceries, I sprinted to the car. As I hurried to dig out the keys and unlock the car doors, the doors of heaven made the most of their head start and blew open wide, dumping buckets of water. The plastic bags seemed to be transformed into miniature rain barrels, as they collected every possible drop of rain that they could!

By the time it was all loaded into the car with some vulnerable items pulled out of the wet bags and my cart returned to the rack, I was thoroughly soaked. I didn't have to worry about my hair being a gooey glob, it was completely washed out by the deluge of water rolling down over my head like a waterfall. Unexpectedly, that initial grumbly attitude had also been rinsed away, and I felt a deep well of release bubbling up from within my soul. It was as if swomething heavy and earthbound was lifting and floating up into the heavenlies. With no hope left to salvage my own prideful self-image, there was an ethereal, peaceful flood of unexplainable joy that began to rise up from within, causing me to laugh and sing all the way home.

In my Father's Book, Mark 10:17-22 tells the parable of the young, rich man who came to Jesus inquiring, "What must I do to inherit eternal life?" He took pride in his faithfulness to have kept all the religious rules and commandments since he was a boy. But he knew that something was missing.

With a heart of compassion, Jesus looked at him lovingly and told him to "Go, sell everything you have and give to the poor, and you will have treasure in heaven. Then come, follow me." The man's face fell, and he sadly walked away, knowing that he couldn't part with his great wealth.

This is one of the stories that I have read many times but have quickly passed over. Wealth has eluded me; Jesus has never asked me to give all that I have away, so why spend time mulling over the passage? Taking a closer look, the Lord began to help me understand that the rich man's prosperity was much more than money and property. Wealth gave him a prominent position in the community. It provided power, dominance and the attention he needed to maintain his inflated self-worth. There's little doubt that he carried pride in his ability to acquire such a luxurious lifestyle. Jesus told him to sell everything and then come follow him. Because his identity and security were so intertwined with his riches, it dominated his life. It powerfully overrode his desire to receive God's spiritual blessings and a future treasure.

When I was about to come under the downpour of a rainfall from heaven, my first reaction was self-preservation. Pridefully, I cared more about people seeing me look like a drowned rat than gracefully accepting what God was sending for me to experience.

God wanted to give me an unexpected time of refreshing amidst my mundane weekly chore. He wanted to call my attention to Himself. "Deep calls out to deep in the roar of your waterfalls; all your waves and breakers have swept over me." Psalm 42:7. I felt the Lord drawing my spirit to His. The roar of heaven's doors opening and pouring out a waterfall was a cleansing rain that washed over me like an ocean wave. There was no escaping the supernatural power that swept over me that day.

"For I will pour water on the thirsty land, and streams on the dry ground..." Isaiah 44:3. God knew what was going on in my life at that very moment. He knew that I had been going through an arid, dry season in my faith. God intervened so that I would get back on track with His agenda for my life. I needed to be spiritually restored.

God wanted to refill me with the joy of my salvation–that wondrous moment of knowing my sins were forgiven and forgotten by God–because Jesus loved me enough to die and pay the price for my redemption. It brought that hallelujah song back to my soul, and my lips couldn't hold back singing praises all the way home. I was "singing in the rain...what a wonderful feeling, I'm happy again..."

LET'S TALK ~ GOD'S HEART FOR YOU

Do you have a song on your lips?

Matthew 12:34 (BSB) says, "For out of the overflow of the heart, the mouth speaks."

In other words, when your heart feels empty, there will be no music coming out of your mouth. If you are enduring a dry, thirsty season like I was experiencing when God intervened, more than likely there will be no praises being spoken either.

My granddaughter is on an eleven-month missionary trip to minister in eleven countries. Somewhat like in the story of the rich man, God called her to give up everything she had to follow Him. She sold her car and invested any money she had into this journey. She has nothing left. Leaving with only a backpack of supplies and clothing, she set out to serve for almost a year with very sparse belongings. She wrote a story on her blog this month, reminding me that we all live through times when we hit a dry spell or feel discouraged, even if we are dramatically walking out God's will. Each month she has asked the Lord to give her a 'word' to meditate on and to guide her actions. I have her permission to share this blog.

A Broken Hallelujah by Samantha Barnhart: (month 7 of the trip)

"My heart is heavy. I feel like the only thing I can do is cry. Even though I may seem to cry more, I still don't like crying, but that is all the strength I can seem to find. This is not what I expected.

Word for the month: Hallelujah (Hebrew)

- *In Hebrew it means: God be praised*
- *In Greek it means: "Praise the Lord"*

How awesome is it for God to give me a word that just means to praise Him? Praising Him is easy when it seems that He is giving you blessing after blessing. A new team, a chance to explore Europe, and being called to Greece! Honestly, it still doesn't seem real. When I shared my new word with my mom, she was excited and could easily see how this is a month to praise Him for the opportunities that are ahead. However, when I shared my word with America (my teammate), her first reaction was to say to praise Him through the storm. I wanted to deny that so quickly. There was no way that He is expecting me to praise Him through the storm in this season.

Here I am, with tears streaming down my face, trying to raise my Hallelujah and praise Him through the storm. I'm tired of the battle. Life at home keeps going on whether I am there or not. My sisters are going through good things and hard things. My church is going through change. I lost my great-grandma. I can see some of the struggles my other friends are going through. I missed my friend's last high school football game, musical and graduation. One of my sweet best friends had her first child and she just learned that her dad only has days to live. All she wants is to be able to hug me and all I want to do is hug her. I am heartbroken and all I can seem to do is cry. I know that being home would not have changed anything but that doesn't mean I'm not wrestling with it.

Lord, why? I don't understand why all this stuff has to happen while I'm not at home. Why do I have to be around the world? Why do I feel so helpless? Why does it hurt so much? Yet, I know that this is where you have called me. I know that you have me in Athens, Greece and on this race for a reason. I know that I can trust in you. So, Lord, with shaking hands and tears streaming down my face I will raise a broken Hallelujah. And I will praise you through the storm." Hallelujah!

Since the beginning of the month when she wrote this, God has been faithful in many ways and her next blog was The Power of a Hallelujah! She testified about God's faithfulness to restore her heart and soul through the storm. She finished up the blog with this ending:

(Samantha's blog) "So, in the darkness you face, shine God.

In the moments in the middle, praise God.
In the highs of life, God is to be praised.
In all seasons of life, boast in God and know that HE is with you."

*Raising your Hallelujah, the glorification of the Lord,
can produce the most powerful effect on us. Raise your
Hallelujah!*

What a powerful testimony of God opening up the heavens and pouring down the rain of restoration over her dry and thirsty soul.

God's heart for you is that you would experience the refreshing waterfall of His Holy Spirit ministering to you throughout whatever season you find yourself in. If you are struggling with great sadness or complicated problems, and all you are able to offer God is a 'Broken Hallelujah', don't hold it back. Give what you are able; God understands. His great love is always with you, even when you aren't feeling it. God's love doesn't depend on whether you feel it or not; it's based on the truth that is found in His Word. Psalm 36:7 says, "How precious is your unfailing love, Oh God!" God promises to watch over you. "The Lord will guide you always; he will satisfy your needs in a sun-scorched land and will strengthen your frame. You will be like a well-watered garden, like a spring whose waters never fail." Isaiah 58:11

God sends His rain to prosper your soul like a well-watered garden that is healthy and thriving by His springs that flow from His throne-room. He wants your heart filled with peace, joy, and wants you filled with the knowledge that you are totally secure in Him. He will guide and satisfy you morning by morning to live a life beyond your circumstances. He will be faithful to rebuild the ruins and the areas that have been broken and damaged in the past. While you are being healed and restored, take your focus off of yourself and your trials, then meditate on the goodness of God. All good and perfect gifts come from the Father above. Be filled with thankfulness, and be grateful for what the Lord is about to do for you. Gloomy days will come, but God still shines so open up your sunshiny-yellow umbrella and start 'singing in the rain.' Praise the Lord despite your circumstances, and raise your Hallelujah!

Reflection: Lord, in what circumstances do I need to raise my Hallelujah?

Meditation music: Raise a Hallelujah (contemporary) or How Great Thou Art (hymn)

5.

TOOL TIME

There's an old television show called Home Improvement that was produced from 1991-1999, and continues even now in syndication. It was about a man who loved to work with tools. He was the main star of a television show sponsored by a tool company. It was a show built within a show. In most episodes of 'Tool Time', you could expect to see him attempting to work on a project that demonstrated a new type or an improved model of a power tool. He always had very good intentions, but the power released in his hands usually brought disaster.

Today as I read through Isaiah chapter 10, it was obvious that God was angry at Israel for their prideful hearts and exalted self-reliance. They had turned away, rejecting His authority over them, to rely on their own worldly wisdom and strength. Therefore, God allowed the foreign nation of Assyria to overpower and conquer them as punishment. Meanwhile, the Assyrians and their king became filled with arrogance because of their accomplishments and military victories. Little did they suspect that they were merely a tool in the hand of God.

Isaiah 10:15 says, "Does the ax raise itself above him who swings it, or the saw boast against him who uses it? As if a rod were to wield him who lifts it up, or a club brandish him who is not wood!" Assyria was proud and boasted of their power but failed to see the true picture. They failed to see who was raising them up and swinging the blow against Israel. They didn't realize that they were about to outlive their usefulness and be discarded by God. When God was finished with them, He pulled the plug. Isaiah 37:36-37 records that 185,000 Assyrian soldiers were slain by the angel of the Lord.

When God raises us up for ministry, we can move forth in faith, knowing that we are the tools that He uses. But sometimes there are periods when God doesn't seem to open the door of opportunities. There have been moments when I have felt like that tool laying on the shelf, slowly corroding and collecting a layer of dust. Last summer, I was feeling as if my life had been tucked into a shed for storage. It seemed as if the most useful, fulfilling, and productive part of my life was over. I agonized about the situation and spent much time seeking the Lord for answers.

It's not clear to me how I reached that point in time where I felt that God was done with my life. Looking back, I have no doubt that, like Assyria, I had some pride issues that God wanted to deal with. It wasn't a boastful haughtiness but a quiet, heart-secret that wasn't hidden from God. Pride can be a sneaky sin. Often, we can recognize it in others long before we see it in ourselves. It can creep in at times when we have worked hard to serve the Lord. But there is a fine line that can be easily crossed. It's okay to feel good about a job well done, as long as we are balanced by the knowledge that God enabled us. It's not a pride problem to look at our lives and be glad that we didn't spend years rebelling against God, as long as we credit it all to God's hand of grace.

Sometimes we may still feel like that tool hanging on the pegboard, oxidizing. Pride isn't always the culprit, often we have just become neglectful in our relationship with God. We become too self-absorbed in life happening around us. At those times of disengagement, we need to ask the Lord to intervene and restore us back to usefulness for His purposes. God will be faithful to rub away the tarnish and complete the work needed to shine us up to effectively serve Him.

Throughout this devotional, I have been questioning the Lord about how the "Tool time" story ties in with what he is showing me. Finally, I understand. It is a caution. Knowing that we are just tools to be used, it is vital that we are aware of the one who attempts to handle us. We have to be able to discern between the Holy Spirit, the human spirit, or a deceiving spirit. Like "Tool time," which was a show within a show, a disaster was always lurking within one of the layers. The tools were never used by the one who designed and created them. Many Godly ministries have fallen when the control shifted. It's important that we never underestimate the tactics of the enemy, who attempts to grab onto every opportunity to defile God's plan.

Keeping ourselves lubricated with the anointing oil of Holy Spirit is the only way to block the oxidizing corrosion of becoming complacent. We do that by obeying God's Holy Word. It tells us to "Devote yourselves to prayer, being watchful and thankful," Colossians 4:2. We need to build our prayer life and learn the scriptures that instruct us, such as Hebrews 4:12, "For the word of God is living and active. Sharper than any double-edged sword, it penetrates even to dividing soul and spirit, joints and marrow; it judges the thoughts and attitudes of the heart." Finally, we need to sit quietly and meditate in His presence, "Be still, and know that I am God;" Psalm 46:10.

It's been four days since Isaiah 10:15 began stirring in my heart, so I began writing out some of my thoughts. What more could God reveal through one verse? Then the Lord shared with me that there is a depth of insight that we can't understand or foresee the existence of before the time that He deems to show us. Although verse 15 clearly spoke of correction and caution, the Lord also speaks a beautiful word of encouragement between the lines. It's a releasing of intimidations that have limited our usefulness in the past.

When our attitude issues have been dealt with, and we know who is controlling us, we are to walk in confidence wherever God leads. There will be times when we find ourselves involved in a ministry or a situation that causes us to question whether our human ability or spiritual gifting will be effective in that area. But like the verse in Isaiah reveals, we are to see ourselves as the ax that God's hand lifts or the saw that He grips to cut through a hard surface–nothing more, but certainly nothing less. Because Christ lives within us, we are already equipped by the presence of the Holy Spirit. There is to be no intimidation by self, others, or Satan that interferes with who God designed and created us to be...His power tools.

"Tool Time" in God's hand is truly a story within a story, existing in multiple layering where disaster doesn't lurk. A series with our Father producing the episodes, will go beyond syndication; it will play into eternity. Will your name be listed in the casting credits?

LET'S TALK ~ GOD'S HEART FOR YOU

There was a movie produced in 1998 called The Truman Show. The film star Jim Carrey played the main character named Truman Burbank, who was adopted and raised by a corporation inside a simulated television show revolving around his life, until he discovered it and decided to escape. Everyone else on the set were actors, including his parents and relatives. Over the years, he would occasionally catch a glimpse of something that was puzzling and didn't seem to make sense. If he questioned it, someone would quickly diffuse the confusion. Those inklings that were stored in Truman's memory bank, however, began adding up to the moment, years later, when he fit the puzzle pieces together and could see a clear picture of what was truth. By then he had lived 30 years of his life in a show within a show, with an audience watching his life play out. Finally, when they saw Truman starting to assemble the truth, many people began rooting for him to escape that world, which was set on an island, surrounded by water to keep him trapped within the borders.

Over the years, as I have studied the Bible, I have put together some clues and puzzle pieces that have revealed a very important truth to me. Our life here on the planet earth is like God's reality show. It resembles a movie set that He created for us to live within the boundaries of this universe. Although we explore outside of this planet, so far, we have been contained to having earth as our home base. Looking through the Scripture, we find evidence that we are aliens in this world and are just passing through. Philippians 3:20 tells us, "But our citizenship is in heaven. And we eagerly await a Savior from there, the Lord Jesus Christ." We were never meant to 'belong' to this world. There's an old Southern gospel song called 'This World is Not My Home,' that my family quartet (my dad, mom, brother and I) used to sing at church social events that makes this clear.

"This world is not my home, I'm just a passing through.
My treasures are laid up, somewhere beyond the blue.
The angels beckon me from heaven's open door,
And I can't feel at home in this world anymore."

God's heart is that you would never feel 'at home' and completely content here, as if this was your forever home. This fallen, cursed earth is only a temporary place where you were born and raised, then given the chance to make your own choice as to whether you will serve and glorify God or reject Him. Serving the Lord requires your willingness to be used by Him. You must long to be like a tool in the confines of His hand, and be prepared at all times to be powered up for a job. God expects you to accomplish every task He sets before you. In Acts 20:24, the Apostle Paul talks about the task as part of a race. "However, I consider my life worth nothing to me; my only aim is to finish the race and complete the task the Lord Jesus has given me—the task of testifying to the good news of God's grace."

In this big arena of life, God will give you fans (fellow Christians) to encourage you. Not only do you have a fan base here, but you have a heavenly fan club. That audience is rooting for you until the time that you escape this world's boundaries and cross the finish line into heaven. Hebrew 12:1 says, "Therefore, since we are surrounded by such a great cloud of witnesses, let us throw off everything that hinders and the sin that so easily entangles. And let us run with perseverance the race marked out for us." The great crowd of witnesses are the saints who have already run their marathon and are now resting on the sidelines. They are joyously sitting in the grandstands of heaven watching this reality show within the eternal show, and they are cheering you on as you power through this life.

Take heart and hang in there, no matter how weary you may become as you run. Don't retire yourself to the shed's shelf or risk oxidizing on a pegboard, while this life of opportunities passes you by. And don't lose 30 years of your life like Truman did, being deceived by a shadowed version of the truth. Keep yourself oiled and spiritually ready to be gripped tightly in the palm of God's hands. Then the echo of heaven's applause will roar as they sit on the edge of their seat to watch as your miraculous series plays out before their eyes. With you alone, a successful syndication would be disastrous and impossible, but with God all things are possible, making for a smash hit at showtime!

Reflection: If you are running the race that God has set before you, you will carry His favor and anointing–touching generations as you trust in Him.

Meditation music: The Blessing or Be Thou My Vision

6.

Enlightened Eyes

The Lord has been urging me to read completely through the Bible again. I had started with the New Testament because it's easier to understand and is always an encouragement in my day. When it was time to move on to the Old Testament, I found myself dragging my feet. Some of those books have so much repetition and lengthy genealogies in them, that I lose my focus and my thoughts drift off. Many of the situations don't seem relevant to modern-day life, at least at first glance. Despite my lack of enthusiasm, I began reading it. Each day I've asked the Lord to show me the things that He wants me to learn and how to apply it to my life. Help me, Lord, to understand how it all fits together.

Finally, my attitude has become one that God can work with, and the Old Testament books are coming alive for me. There are still sections that I'm tempted to scan over, but He tells me, "No." Besides learning some of the more obvious truths and lessons in there, sometimes unusual things seem to jump off the pages.

In Numbers 22:21-31, there is a very strange story about Balaam and his donkey. Balaam was a sorcerer, a non-Israelite prophet. He truly heard from God, but his heart was not right with God. He acknowledged that Yahweh (the Lord) was a powerful god; but he also believed in many other gods. The king of Moab sent messengers with money to pay Balaam to put a curse on the Israelites. So Balaam saddled his donkey and left with his two servants. God was very angry when he went along with the king's men, and the angel of the Lord stood in the road to oppose him. Verse 23 reads, "When the donkey saw the angel of the LORD standing in the road with a drawn sword in his hand, *she* turned off the path and went into a field."

As I continued to read the rest of the story, what stood out to me was the fact that God allowed the donkey to see in the spiritual realm. Three times *she* saw the angel with the drawn sword and turned to avoid death. Balaam was angry and beat the donkey each time. Then the Lord opened the donkey's mouth to speak to Balaam twice. Verse 31 says, "Then the Lord opened Balaam's eyes and he saw the angel of the LORD standing in the road with a drawn sword in his hand. And Balaam bowed low and fell facedown."

When I read this, I realized that I could relate to that donkey. Not only is the donkey referred to as a *she*, but the donkey's life somewhat parallels mine at times. It seems a little degrading, but here is what the Lord has shown me. Like Balaam's donkey, I am pretty content to go through my normal daily tasks. Sometimes my stubborn streak rears up, and I refuse to move in a new direction unless He blocks my current road. I may even "hee-haw" (rebel) and go off in the wrong direction. More than those easy-to-see traits, what I found most interesting is the fact that God used that lowly donkey in an unconceivable way. God opened the eyes of the donkey three times to see into the spiritual realm. He enlightened her eyes. Then God opened the donkey's mouth twice and gave her words to speak.

Not long ago, God started to do something a little different in my life. At Bible study, we always start with a time of worship. One morning while we were singing and praying, God showed me a visual picture. A little later during prayer time, God pressed on my heart to speak and share what He was showing me. I wasn't very compliant and my stubborn reluctance kept my mouth shut as I inwardly questioned God. "What would everyone think of me? No, I'm not doing it; I'm way too shy. I don't want any attention. Is this really of You, God? Do I have to do this?" My will was having a tug-of-war with God's will. But God wouldn't release me from what He wanted me to do. I began to tremble and my heart started to pound. Finally, God opened this donkey's mouth and I spoke the words He gave me, and I shared the vision.

For a long time, I struggled every time God did that to me. I was content to be quiet, where I was comfortable. I didn't really want to move in a new direction unless I faced the angel of the LORD with a drawn sword...and had no other option. Often, I went to Bible study with a pre-determination not to open my mouth. But meanwhile, I spent a lot of time in prayer asking for affirmation from God. Seeking Him helped me to trust and understand what He was doing. God was enlightening my eyes. He was opening up the eyes of my heart and pouring out His love and thoughts through me. He was giving me words to speak to encourage other believers—words to uplift them and to remind them that we have an unshakable hope in Jesus Christ.

When you spend time with God, don't be surprised or feel nervous if He shows you a visual picture, or if He gives you words to share with someone. God is just wanting to open the eyes of your heart so that He can use you for His purpose. You are not only to be His hands and feet in this world, but also His voice. Pray and be sure it is coming from God and then obey. As a safe-guard, I have asked God to put His foot on my tongue when I am not to speak.

In Ephesians 1:17-18, I love these encouraging words God used to confirm this new thing that He was doing in my life. The Apostle Paul wrote this passage to all believers. "I keep asking that the God of our Lord Jesus Christ, the glorious Father, may give you the Spirit of wisdom and revelation, so that you may know him better. I pray also that the eyes of your heart may be enlightened in order that you may know the hope to which he has called you, the riches of his glorious inheritance in the saints, and his incomparably great power for us who believe."

LET'S TALK ~ GOD'S HEART FOR YOU

Truthfully, can you relate to Balaam's donkey in any aspects? Do you have some stubbornness, a fear of swords, or are you motivated by self-survival? Has there ever been a detour blocking your path, forcing you to move in a new direction? Well, I can relate! Early this morning, I planned to write this wrap-up section until I realized that I had an eye appointment scheduled. Don't you hate when your plans get interrupted? I had to go in a different direction, and I wasn't happy about it until a crazy thing started to happen. While I was getting ready to leave for my eye exam, God started showing me what to write.

My husband drove me to the eye doctor since the eye drops really affect my vision. I have a complication that makes it worse. Eighteen months ago, I had a stroke in my right eye. A speck of plaque traveled to a vessel in the bottom half of my eye. It blocked the blood flow, and the cells in that area died. The damage can't be repaired. Because the lens of the eye flips your vision, I have a blind area like an umbrella on the top half of my eye, which throws my balance off. Sometimes I depend on a cane or others to help me.

This morning God was showing me that a lot of the time our vision is impaired as if we've had eye drops or a mini stroke. The clarity of our own eyesight is blurred when we are not seeing life through God's eyes. If the eyes of our hearts aren't connecting to the spiritual realm of His heart, there will be a blind spot in our vision that will throw our balance off. If we don't learn to access God's blessing of provision, we will never see with 'enlightened eyes.' According to Webster's dictionary, provision means: the act or process of providing, a measure taken beforehand to deal with a need: PREPARATION. God has pro-VISION and SEES ahead of time what we need. He has already taken measures to provide for us physically and spiritually in advance. The preparation work has been done; His provision is ready and waiting for us.

Paul writes in Ephesians 1:3, "Praise be to the God and Father of our Lord Jesus Christ, who has blessed us in the heavenly realms

36

with every spiritual blessing in Christ." Later in verse 18 Paul writes, "I pray also that the eyes of your heart may be enlightened in order that you may know the hope to which he has called you..."

Those two Scriptures are definitely tied together; they are in the same passage. God has already prepared every spiritual blessing in the heavenly realm for us to access. These are full sentences, not just a few words randomly picked out to form anything out of context. Paul's heart was for believers to know that the "eyes of our heart may be enlightened" so we can fully understand the hope and the commission that God has called us to undertake.

Romans 12:1-2 tells us, "Therefore, I urge you, brothers and sisters, in view of God's mercy, to offer your bodies as a living sacrifice, holy and pleasing to God—this is your true and proper worship. Do not conform to the pattern of this world, but be transformed by the renewing of your mind. Then you will be able to test and approve what God's will is—his good, pleasing and perfect will." When we offer ourselves to God as a living sacrifice, holy and pleasing to God, that is true and proper worship. That is what pleases the Lord. Offering to lay down our life, our will, and our preferences to serve and obey is an act of holiness before God. We are not to be so conformed to the world and its viewpoint that we fail to be transformed with spiritually-renewed minds.

Chapter 12 continues on to list spiritual gifts given to believers to encourage and minister within the body of Christ. Verses 6-8 "We have different gifts, according to the grace given to each of us. If your gift is prophesying, then prophesy in accordance with your faith; if it is serving, then serve; if it is teaching, then teach; if it is to encourage, then give encouragement; if it is giving, then give generously; if it is to lead, do it diligently; if it is to show mercy, do it cheerfully."

These gifts are empowered by the Holy Spirit at a level that is humanly impossible to achieve. God's Heart for you is that the 'eyes of your heart would be enlightened' so that you would see more clearly into the spiritual realm to receive insight. God's desire is that you would flourish in whatever the Holy Spirit commissions you to do or say. His Spirit that lives inside you is the source of that flow between you and God's Heart. According to 1 Corinthians

2:13, "When we tell you these things, we do not use words that come from human wisdom. Instead, we speak words given to us by the Spirit, using the Spirit's words to explain spiritual truths."

That may seem hard to grasp. But remember, Romans 12:2 tells us we are being transformed by the renewing of our minds. The ultimate goal set before us is this "We understand these things, for we have the mind of Christ." 1 Corinthians 2:15b. We need to have the mind of Christ. That's what the Scripture says. Do not underestimate the plans God has for you because of a limited, human mind that limits what is possible with God. You are to be living with a fully developed sense of the Holy Spirit of God, who dwells in you.

In humbleness before Him, open the door of your understanding and realize that the Lord wants to reign through your life in His supernatural power. Your life was never meant to be 'all about you,' but instead, you were meant to bring glory to the Lord. Allow the Spirit of God to flow freely. Open the eyes of your heart and be 'enlightened.' Then, like Balaam's lowly donkey, you will be perfectly fit to be used by God in the most incredible, inconceivable ways!

Reflection: Am I willing to let God open the eyes of my heart to see Him more clearly?

Meditation music: Open the Eyes of My Heart or Open My Eyes, That I May See

7.

Bird in a Cage

There is a beautiful cockatiel that lives in our house. He is mostly yellow with some gray feathers on his wings. He has a little bit of white on him and an orange blush coloring on each cheek. About two years ago, he was given to my son. After a week, my son moved the bird from his bedroom to the living room. He was tired of being awakened early every morning. "Tweeters" has the vocal ability to wake up the dead. Not only is he annoyingly loud, but he has a nasty bite.

When I realized that this bird had been passed over to me to feed and care for, I decided to begin by getting him to trust me. Day after day for weeks, I hand fed him sunflower seeds, one at a time. I would hold each one into the cage close enough for him to reach and bite the seed, but not my fingers. After a few minutes of that, I would put a scoop of mixed seeds in his dish. Gradually, Tweeters was less afraid and began to like me. Many times, if we forgot to put the extra clamp on the cage door, he was smart enough to unlatch it and let himself out.

Before long, this little bird began to search for me every time he escaped from the cage. Tweeters would fly around the house endlessly until he found me. He would fly over to me, perch on my shoulder, and begin to whistle and sing in my ear. I would whistle back at him. He was happy to sit there for as long as I would let him. One day when he found me, not only did he sing to me but while perched on my shoulder, he began pulling strands of my hair through his beak. I thought, "What is he doing?" Then I realized that Tweeters was cleaning my "feathers" just like he cared for his own. He would have been content to stay there forever. That is the day I knew how much he loved me.

In the Bible, Solomon was the king of Israel. He was endowed by God with such incredible wisdom that foreigners came to sit at his feet to learn and glean his knowledge. The king loved God and built a magnificent temple for Him. When it was completed, the people of Israel assembled together and Solomon dedicated it to the Lord. In 1 Kings 8:56-61, Solomon praised the Lord for all that He had done for the people. Then he prayed that the Lord would be with them as He was with their fathers. Solomon prayed that God would turn their hearts to Him, to walk in His ways and to keep all His commands. The king asked the Lord to take care of their daily needs so that all the people in the world would know that the Lord is God and there is no other.

Verse 61 says "But your hearts must be fully committed to the Lord our God, to live by His decrees and obey His commands, as at this time." This verse seemed to throw in some stipulations for the blessing spoken by Solomon to remain in effect. The words 'fully committed' looked like key words. Some Bible versions used words such as perfect, loyal, wholly true, and wholly devoted. The king and the nation embraced the blessing and they followed after God for a while.

Over time, Solomon married foreign women, mostly to secure political alliances. These beautiful, wealthy wives brought their pagan gods with them. Solomon thought that he was too wise to ever be influenced by their practices. But gradually, his love for these women wove an invisible 'cage' around his heart as he was caught up in love's allure. He succumbed to their persistence to worship with them. He even built elaborate shrines to honor their gods.

King Solomon's devotion to God became divided, then it faltered. He did what was evil in the Lord's sight. His disobedient mindset spurned habitual sin, dumbed-down his wisdom, and numbed his heart toward the One true God. No longer was he 'fully committed' or wholly devoted. The people followed his example and pursued other gods. Therefore, God removed His blessing over the king and the nation of Israel.

Tweeters is visibly a "bird in a cage." Usually, he has no way of escape. If given a choice, nothing within the bars could attract him to stay, not even his love for sunflower seeds and fresh food. So many days I see myself like that bird; trapped. I'm surrounded by an invisible net of work, pressures, and other people's demands for my time. It can be an everyday snare if I'm not wise enough to plan my daily escape.

I am reminded of the devotion of that little bird. He is single-minded, 'fully committed', and wholly true. Every chance he gets, he flies to me and expresses his delight and love. Can I say the same about my own mindset? Do I run to my Father and sit at His feet, content to stay as long as possible? Over the years, God has taught me to trust him, seed by seed, as he cares for me. We have walked together through many things in life. Yet sometimes, He is not my first priority. Like Solomon, are there other loves or things in my life that are so alluring that my devotion to God becomes divided?

Tweeters instinctively comes to me, without fail. He doesn't stop looking until he finds me. Even with a tiny bird-brain, he has enough wisdom to know who cares for him and where his security lies. Others in this house have threatened to find him a new home, but that is not in my plan. Because Tweeters has made his love for me so obvious, he has touched my heart. He will always be far from perfect, but we are devoted and find delight in each other.

God's heart is to love us, to bless us, and to be in an intimate relationship with us. We will always be far from perfect, but the

Bible declares that God takes delight in us. Psalm 149:4 says, "For the Lord takes delight in His people, He crowns the humble with salvation." Psalm 37:4 encourages each of us, "Delight yourself in the Lord; And He will give you the desires of your heart."

Understanding the extent of our Father's love and affection for us, how can we knowingly offer Him so much less?

LET'S TALK ~ GOD'S HEART FOR YOU

If you lived 2,000 years ago and Jesus came to your house, how would you react and what would you do?

In the Bible there is a story about two sisters, Mary and Martha. One day Jesus came to visit them. They were both so excited to see Him. Immediately, Martha probably offered Him something to drink. Then she bustled around in the kitchen to prepare a delicious meal for Jesus. Meanwhile, Mary never showed up in the kitchen to help her sister, which irritated Martha. So, as Martha's temper began stewing, along with the food, she finally had to find and confront Mary. Stomping into the living area, she found her sister. Mary was sitting at Jesus' feet and was listening to every word He spoke. Martha angrily complained to Jesus about Mary not helping her. "Martha, Martha," the Lord answered, "You are worried and upset about many things, but few things are needed-or indeed only one. Mary has chosen what is better, and it will not be taken away from her."

You see, Mary loved with an undivided heart-like my bird Tweeters. Her love for Jesus exceeded her need for anything else in this world. Mary's kind of love brought her to sit at Jesus' feet. She hung onto every word He spoke, as if her devotion to Him was magnetized. Mary's heart was undivided and set on things above. Martha loved Jesus too, yet her love for being recognized as a proper, respectable hostess over-rode her devotion for Him.

Right now, on the mission field, my granddaughter Samantha is with a young adult team in Indonesia. One of her best friends, Hunter, recently blogged his intense insight about God's love and grace. Try to put yourself in this reflection of undivided love. With his permission, I will share it with you.

(Hunter's blog)

"At any moment, no matter where I'm at, no matter what I've just done, no matter where my heart currently stands or how distracted it may be, in each moment God looks down on me with extreme and utmost love and says, "I love you, Hunter". When I pause to think on these words being spoken by the God of the universe to me, I think of the joy that it is to walk in this reality. And it is reality.

At any moment, He is deeply in love with me and desires to be with me. In no way do I mean to demean or belittle God in saying this, but what if I saw that God was just a little obsessed with me. I mean that He yearns and craves to spend time with me and just longs for the moment that I come to Him and sit with Him. Talk to Him. Listen to Him. Nothing fancy. He just wants to be with me. He just wants my heart.

What if, in a way, I saw God as just a little bit desperate for me. I do not mean any disrespect and it honestly feels a bit odd writing this. But I don't mean that He needs us. When I think of the word desperate, I think of someone who will go to any length, pay any cost, sacrifice anything, to complete his/her purpose. And if they are truly desperate, they will do anything! Sounds a lot like what God did for us. He was willing to do anything and He did. I by no means believe God is desperate for us in that He is dependent on us, but might He just be a bit desperate for us to know Him? I mean He gave everything and that which was most precious to Him just to have a relationship with us. He deeply craves and longs for a relationship with us. He gave EVERYTHING.

The whole story of the Bible, the whole narrative of creation and existence itself is so that man would know and have a relationship with God. There was a disruption in this through sin, but the beauty of the Gospel is that He gave up EVERYTHING to restore that relationship with the ones (you and me) that He loves most. And more, what if we had just a bit of that same desperation for Him? What if I, Hunter Beck, could see how radical and extreme God's love is for me and dwelt on this on a more continual basis? What freedom and grace I would walk in every single day. "For freedom, I have been set free" (Galatians 5:1). I feel I'd be walking on clouds, breathing in the sunshine, head a little higher and smile a little brighter. Man, we truly are so deeply loved when we take a moment to pause and reflect on it. His grace is so over-the-top and abundant. It washes over us at every moment. It is always accessible. God truly is love."

God's Heart for you is that you would grasp what is most important in this life. Hunter has chosen to live in the realm of the love and grace of God right now. 2,000 years ago, Jesus said that Mary had chosen better-she had an undivided heart of love for Jesus. Nothing compared, distracted, or could compete with her depth of devotion. Mary's heart delighted in the Lord. Psalms 149:4 says, "For the Lord takes delight in His people, He crowns the humble with salvation." The Lord delights in you when you put Him first in your life. Know that you are deeply loved by God. Escape from the birdcage that keeps you trapped in the net of distractions. Christ has the key that unlocks the door for you to live daily in freedom and grace. Come to Jesus and engage in a radical, 'fully committed,' devoted relationship together. Like Hunter shared, you will walk on clouds, breathe in the sunshine, hold your head a little higher, and smile a little brighter!

Reflection: Knowing that God's love for me is radical and extreme, am I fully committed and devoted to Him?

Meditation music: Nothing Else or I Am Thine, O Lord

8.

A VACANT FENCE

For the past week, I have been reading through I Kings and 2 Kings in the Old Testament. There is a lot of information in the Scripture about the kings of the Jewish nation of Israel and Judah, and the surrounding pagan nations. I Kings begins at the end of King David's reign. Overall, David was a good king, yet we know that he was not without sin. When he was confronted with it, he earnestly repented from the evil he had committed. David was the only king who was referred to as "a man after God's own heart."

There were many kings that the scripture described with these words "and he (the king) did evil in the eyes of the Lord." Many of these kings, along with the people, practiced pagan rituals including the horrendous sacrifice of children.

Other kings were described with the words "He did right in the eyes of the Lord. The high places, however, were not removed; the people continued to offer sacrifices and burned incense there." On one hand those kings would follow after God in their own lives, yet on the other hand, they allowed the pagan shrines and worship places to remain. They had the authority and power to destroy them, but for some reason they were unwilling to exert the effort. Maybe those kings couldn't change the people's hearts, but why didn't they take a more deliberate stand for God? Wasn't it their kingdom to reign over?

When I was studying these books, I thought, "Why in the world would God put up with the wickedness in the nation of His own people?" I thought about how awful it must have been to live there and how thankful I am to live in America, a nation which was founded under God.

Today, before I opened my Bible to finish reading the end of 2 Kings, I started to think about the many heart-breaking crises that have been happening in our country. Actually, our nation doesn't seem much different than those evil nations that I have been reading about. Maybe we have spent too much time sitting on the fence, just like some of those kings who knew right from wrong but didn't stand up for God's righteousness to rule in every area of life. Although we are not officially appointed kings, what would be required of us to become 'a man (or woman) after God's own heart' like King David?

You know, I always believed that I was following God with my whole heart, yet have I been too silent when it comes to the sinful practices of people around me? At times I've been guilty of holding my tongue and only shaking my head in disgust, when I should have lovingly shared the truth of God's Word with people.

During some elections I became so annoyed with the political mud-slinging that I stayed home and didn't vote. Instead of taking the time to search the background record of the candidates to see who lined up best with God's standards, I sat on the fence with my feet pulled up, resting on the railing, and I didn't support either side.

2 Kings 16:3 said that Ahaz, King of Israel, sacrificed his son in the fire. Some of the evil kings not only allowed child sacrifice, but they joined in with the pagan rituals and killed some of their own. It's hard to comprehend anything that could be so extremely evil. Yet, that's happening here in our nation, literally, through legal abortion up to the moment of birth. Most of us

detest that horrible law and have been praying for years for it to be overturned.

But there are other ways in which the spiritual welfare of our children has been sacrificed. Through our negligence, we may have thrown our children to wolves dressed in sheep's clothing. We might have been carelessly persuaded at times to let our kids engage in activities where their innocence and moral standards were slowly being corrupted by uncensored electronics, inappropriate movies, tv, and unsavory social media.

The Lord has been showing me that many times I was so busy trying to finish chores without distraction that I pushed my children away. It wasn't unusual for me to tell them to go watch tv or go play their video games. Often, I didn't pay attention to the content. Who knew that you could no longer trust the morals portrayed even in many of the Disney produced programs? Their subtle twisting of God's standard has been so cleverly disguised that it's easy to miss if you are not paying close attention. It can seep into a corner in our children's minds and eventually become a rebellious voice that sways them from righteous thinking.

God continued to speak to my heart about times when I ignored our kid's music booming in their rooms. Shrugging off their choice of music style as being basically harmless was letting my spiritual guard down. God has given us discernment through the Holy Spirit to even decipher questionable Christian lyrics and the intention of that artist. As they unknowingly absorb deceptive concepts, seeds can be planted in the listener's subconscious that later may grow into standards that do not line up with God's precepts written in His Word.

Looking back now, how did I not realize that my own good intentions were somewhat unbalanced? Sometimes I was so self-absorbed with my own spiritual need to find time every day for devotional moments with God that I failed to notice my children had that same need. Yes, I read them Christian stories and we prayed, but I didn't encourage them enough to also learn how to do it on their own. God has been showing me that unless a parent sets that as a priority, it will not just happen. Children need our time and supervision to help them grow in their faith. We need to exert the effort to guide them while they are living under our roof. Like the Godly responsibility of the kings of the past, isn't this our kingdom to reign over?

Most of the time I prefer to finish my stories with a sweet, feel-good ending, and I could easily sit on the fence with my feet propped up so that I don't cause offense. But I'm being booted to vacate it and stand up on the side of God's Word. He's reminded me of the passage in Revelation 3:15-16 about the church in Laodicea: "I know your deeds, that you are neither cold nor hot. I wish you were either one or the other! So, because you are lukewarm—neither hot nor cold—I am about to spit you out of my mouth." We are repulsive to God when we have a foot dangling on each side of the fence and remain lukewarm. God has revealed truth, and I know that I am accountable for the wisdom of knowing good from evil. He has made it known to me; I am without excuse when it comes to choosing sides and recognizing which side God wants me to align myself with.

Revelation 3:19-20 goes on to say, "Those whom I love I rebuke and discipline. So be earnest and repent. Here I am! I stand at the door and knock. If anyone hears my voice and opens the door, I will come in and eat with that person, and they with me." The Lord rebuked and disciplined me for my lack of taking the responsibility that He had entrusted to me when I was raising my children. Like King David, my heart is grieved by my actions, and for any of the ways it might have affected their lives.

The Lord was knocking on my heart's door this morning because it was time for that area to be reconciled and my sin forgiven. When He looks at my life, God will see a vacant fence, because I have chosen to exert my spiritual authority over this earthly kingdom, and stand up for righteousness. Sweet fellowship with my Lord has been restored, and I feel blessed to be in His presence. "Blessed are those whose ways are blameless; who walk according to the law of the Lord. Blessed are those who keep his statutes and seek him with all their heart." Psalm 119:1-2

LET'S TALK ~ GOD'S HEART FOR YOU

In the very center of the Bible, we find the book of Psalms. The longest chapter in the entire Bible is Psalm 119, which has 176 verses. Therefore, this chapter must certainly contain information that is vital to living our lives as Christians. If I were to write a subtitle of its message into one sentence, it would be: The Secret of Living a Blessed Life that Glorifies God. Doesn't that make you want to start reading it right away? If it does, then you should. Within the book you will find many familiar verses such as vs.105 (KJV), "Thy word is a lamp unto my feet, and a light unto my path."

God inspires the unknown writer of Psalm 119 to explain that obeying God's laws, decrees, standards, statues, precepts, and commands gives you the ability to walk in the freedom that was given to you at the moment of your salvation. It was a phenomenal freedom that came at a great price; it cost Christ His life. From that time, we have been like babes learning to walk in that remarkable gift. But sometimes the lack of the knowledge and understanding of God's word has bound our feet from moving in the power and righteous boldness that God expects us to have achieved by this point in our spiritual maturity.

The basis for my thoughts is found in verses 41-47. "May your unfailing love come to me, Lord, your salvation, according to your promise; then I can answer anyone who taunts me, for I trust in your word. Never take your word of truth from my mouth, for I have put my hope in your laws. I will always obey your law, for ever and ever. I will walk about in freedom, for I have sought out your precepts. I will speak of your statutes before kings and will not be put to shame for I delight in your commands because I love them."

God's heart for you is that you would always walk in His ways, His truth, and in freedom from all the deception going on in this world. It is not easy to do unless you are willing to meditate daily on His Word. Even then, God knows that you will never be perfect, but He will know that you long for Him to see you as a man or woman after His own heart. God has a life for you that requires you to be diligent in your integrity and ready to obediently respond when He nudges your heart into action. It may be in the area of raising your family, in the workplace arena, or even supporting a person in an election that isn't afraid to publicly mention God. Political correctness is not a mandate from God and most often is in direct opposition to His word. Search it out for yourself. When the Lord looks at your life, will He see you taking a bold stand for His kingdom beside a vacant fence, or will you still be on the top rail with your feet propped up to avoid a life-changing decision and commitment? Choose wisely..."Show me Your ways, Lord; Teach me Your paths. Guide me in your truth and teach me, for you are my God my Savior, and my hope is in you all day long." Psalms 25:4-5

Reflection: Lord, is there an area in my life where I need to exert my spiritual authority and stand up for righteousness?

Meditation music: Call Upon the Lord (Elevation Worship) or Stand Up, Stand Up for Jesus

9.

Joshua Stones

Recently, I was awakened during the night by my husband laughing. He got up, left the room, and came back a few minutes later. As I laid in bed, in the dark, with my eyes still closed, I could hear a scraping noise across the bed sheet. The scraping noise continued, so finally I said "What are you doing, and why were you laughing?" He replied "I woke up with stuff around my face and mouth. As I was pulling and poofing it away from my mouth, I realized my pillow had burst and I was laying in a pile of feathers! I'm scraping them up and putting them back in my pillow." I chuckled then went back to sleep.

It was still dark when my alarm went off a few hours later. I'm not a morning person, so I didn't turn on any lights as I walked down the hallway to the kitchen. Then I turned on the dim light over the stove and sink. As my son was getting ready for school, I briefly explained why there were feathers on the bathroom floor and sink.

Later in the morning, I went to Bible study. When we gathered at the table with our coffee and snack, I giggled as I pictured my husband pulling all those feathers away from his mouth and out of his full beard and hair. Of course, the ladies wanted to know what was so funny, so I explained what had happened during the night. Then I told them that I was standing in the kitchen when my husband suddenly reached around me and started plucking feathers from the back of my hair.

That's when I had begun to realize the extent of the feathery mess I would find in the bedroom. After he left for work, I had followed a trail of feathers back the hallway. The bed spread had a few on the top of it but when I lifted the blankets, they were everywhere. I told the ladies that I still had all that mess to clean up when I returned home. Before my husband walked out the door, he had said, "Please, don't sweep them all up into the sweeper." I had to promise to pick them up and restuff those feathers back into his pillow because they were from chickens that his grandmother had raised and plucked! We were all laughing.

Now as I think about it, I realize that the feather pillow is so much more than what it appears to be. In a sense, it is a memorial to the love and hard work of his grandmother. For him, it's a reminder of the past and the wonderful memories he treasures even now, many, many years later.

Reading through the Old Testament, there were many times altars were built as memorials. In Genesis 33:20, Jacob built an altar and called it "El Elohe Israel" which means Mighty God of Israel. In Genesis 35:7, Jacob built another altar and called it "El Bethel" meaning God of Bethel–a holy place, house of God. Moses built and named one "The Lord is my Banner" in Exodus 17:15. Joshua chapter 22 tells about several tribes of Israel building an imposing altar called "A Witness Between Us that the Lord is God." It was a memorial for the people to remember that they all worshipped the same God. It was a sign of unity between the tribes. It was never used for sacrifices.

One of the most significant memorials that I have read about happened in Joshua 4. When it was God's time for Joshua to take the Israelites into the Promised Land, the priests were to lead the procession and carry the Ark of the Covenant. As they stepped into the Jordan, God parted the waters, just as he had parted the Red Sea for their ancestors. The priests stood, holding the ark in the middle of the dry river bed as the people crossed. Afterwards, Joshua sent a man from each of the twelve tribes to go back to the place where the priests held the ark. They were to bring back twelve large stones, each carrying one on their shoulder.

Then Joshua set up those twelve stones as a memorial to God for His mighty, powerful, and supernatural acts. It was to help the people focus on God as he led them to possess the land and in the battles that were still before them. It was a visible reminder to tell their children and the next generations of God's great deeds.

What an impact it would make in our own lives if we would begin to set up visible memorials of God's Hand. If we would faithfully write about the times when God has protected us, provided extra money to pay bills, or has brought us through an illness, we would be building a lasting memorial to God's greatness. Our personal stories would be a great source of hope and encouragement when we faced other difficult times—not only for us but for our family generations. To clearly remember God's work and faithfulness in the past would strengthen our spiritual muscle to be able to push through whatever we face. Challenging our children to look at ways God is working in their lives and helping them set up a visual memorial would be a faith builder. It would be a lasting reminder of God's love and hand in their lives.

Not too long ago, God showed me a visual picture of the cover of a devotional book that I would be writing to help support a new ministry. I said to God, "What would I ever find to write a whole book about?" Then my eyes landed on my journal and God said "Those things that I have been teaching you and will be teaching you." For the past year, I have been faithfully journaling, for my own benefit, about things God has pressed upon my heart.

As God began to take those things and show me how to write about them for this book, they were like the Joshua stones. Each devotion that was completed was a visible reminder of God's mighty hand. It wasn't my hand; I'm not a writer. At times when I began to wonder if God would ever show me enough to fill a book, I would look over the stories that were finished. I saw His work and I was encouraged. Then, I could refocus on God and trust that He was leading me. God goes before me in all my endeavors, and he fights my battles that often come as an attempt to destroy his plan.

The silly, but true, story of my husband's feathery experience and that important memorial, that he had subconsciously set up to honor his grandmother, is an example that our family will never forget. How much more important are the memorials we set up to honor God. They will strengthen our faith and build our trust in God. Those visual reminders of God's mighty deeds will be unforgettable stepping stones in our relationship with our Father. Psalms 145:1-7 says:

> I will exalt you, my God the King;
> I will praise your name for ever and ever.
> Every day I will praise you
> and extol your name for ever and ever.
> Great is the Lord and most worthy of praise;
> his greatness no one can fathom.
> One generation commends your works to another;
> they tell of your mighty acts.
> They speak of the glorious splendor of your majesty,
> and I will meditate on your wonderful works.
> They tell of the power of your awesome works,
> and I will proclaim your great deeds.
> They celebrate your abundant goodness
> and joyfully sing of your righteousness.

LET'S TALK ~ GOD'S HEART FOR YOU

What memorials have you set up in your home? A memorial is an object which serves as a focus for a memory of something like a special event, or of a person who has died. Many of us have old pictures of relatives or things in our house that were passed down through our family to us. Those things mean a lot to us because they recall special memories.

In my house, I have a picture on my wall that has a map of Africa, with a lion, an elephant, and a giraffe along the left side of it. When I glance at it, I'm reminded of how God took care of my nineteen-year-old granddaughter when she traveled alone to Mozambique to serve with a missionary organization for three months. While she was gone, it reminded me to pray. Now, after hearing her stories—one about walking under a tree branch that a poisonous black mamba was laying on, ready to strike out at her—I'm reminded to praise God for His mighty acts of protection over her life.

A memorial in the Bible was significant. It was based on the concept of remembering God and God remembering us. It was a "remembrance" that could be marked by a visible "sign" such as the rainbow. In the Old Testament, we find the story of Noah and the flood. Afterwards God set up an unforgettable memorial sign of a great promise, a covenant.

Genesis 9:12-16 "And God said, "This is the sign of the covenant I am making between me and you and every living creature with you, a covenant for all generations to come: I have set my rainbow in the clouds, and it will be the sign of the covenant between me and the earth. Whenever I bring clouds over the earth and the rainbow appears in the clouds, I will remember my covenant between me and you and all living creatures of every kind. Never again will the waters become a flood to destroy all life. Whenever the rainbow appears in the clouds, I will see it and remember the everlasting covenant between God and all living creatures of every kind on the earth."

In the New Testament, the Lord's Supper was set up by Jesus as a lasting memorial. It says in 1 Corinthians 11:24-25: And when He had given thanks, he (Jesus) broke it and said, "This is my body, which is for you; do this in remembrance of me." In the same way, after supper he took the cup, saying, "This cup is the new covenant in my blood; do this, whenever you drink it, in remembrance of me." This was initiated so that we would remember that God's redeeming gift of salvation came through the sacrifice of His Precious Son.

God's heart for you is that you always remember His great and mighty deeds throughout your life. Ask God to lead you to find ways to commemorate His love and faithfulness. It would be a wonderful source of encouragement for you, your family, and your friends. Create your own Joshua Stones Family Journal as a memorial book (a notebook or journal) designated to record the miracles and amazing things that God has done on your behalf. It would be a book of remembrance of God's supernatural acts that you and your family have witnessed over the years. Just like God told Joshua to set up twelve stones to be a visible reminder, we also need visible reminders that God is powerful.

Psalm 71:18 "Even when I am old and gray, do not forsake me, my God, till I declare your power to the next generation, your mighty acts to all who are to come."

Psalm 77:11 "I will remember the deeds of the LORD; yes, I will remember your miracles of long ago. I will consider all your words and meditate on all your mighty deeds. Your ways, God, are holy. What god is as great as our God? You are the God who performs miracles; you display your power among the peoples."

Often, as adults, we have many memories of miracles, and of God pulling us through difficult times or tragedies. God reminds us in Scripture about the importance of telling our children and grandchildren, the next generation, just as He commanded the Israelites to do. Writing it down would keep the story intact and precise instead of relying on our sometimes-faulty memories. Take this challenge as a new hobby that will make every minute you spend on it significant. It will be well worth your time and energy. Through the inspiration of the Holy Spirit, this remembrance may give hope to many and perhaps lead them to salvation. Telling our stories is a powerful encouragement for our families, so they can see how God worked in us and protected our spiritual heritage. Our legacy of faith, filled with our Father's wisdom, is the most valuable gift we can give them. Isn't that an exciting possibility?

Reflection: What memorable deeds has the Lord done in your life that need to be recorded to encourage others?

Meditation music: If I Told You My Story or Redeemed

10.

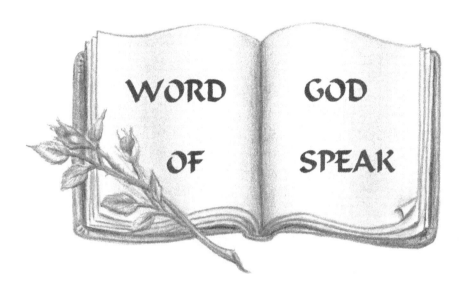

WORD   GOD

OF   SPEAK

At the beginning of each new year, a friend of mine reads the Bible until God shows her a specific verse or passage for her to meditate on throughout the year. One year, God led her to Isaiah 50:4 "The Sovereign LORD has given me a well-instructed tongue, to know the word that sustains the weary. He wakens me morning by morning, wakens my ear to listen like one being taught."

As she began to meditate on it, she kept thinking about me and knew that the Lord wanted her to share it with me. When I looked it up in my Bible, I read it but also continued to read through verse 5. "The Sovereign LORD has opened my ears, and I have not been rebellious; I have not drawn back."

Honestly, I know that I have the tendency to be slightly rebellious, especially when someone tells me to do something or say something in a specific way. I will reluctantly do it, although I really want to do it my way. Even when God tells me to do something, I sometimes want to slightly alter it so I am not stretched beyond my comfort zone of my own ability. It was obvious this verse was indeed for me. God wanted me to meditate and hold onto these particular verses throughout all He was about to do in and through my life that year.

God had already been calling my heart to complete obedience. One area of obedience was in journaling through the Word and writing down whatever He was speaking to me through it. I was to journal whenever I sensed and knew God was moving my heart during prayer, sermons, and even through music. He was setting me on a course with a specific plan and purpose.

That journaling was intense and very time consuming, but I had promised God...my obedience. Journaling everything that He pressed on my heart was like seeing pieces of a life puzzle scattered on a table. One by one, each written promise, thought, revelation was being developed and transferred from the Spiritual realm to my own spirit realm. Except for these tiny clues–puzzle pieces, I had no vision of the picture God was creating for my life. At that time, I had no idea how to connect the pieces together. It was beyond my own understanding.

Faithfully I wrote. I remember one unusual entry after reading the story about Balaam and his donkey. At some point in the story, the female donkey saved their life when God open her eyes to see the angel of the LORD standing in the road with a drawn sword in his hand. Then the LORD opened the donkey's mouth to speak to Balaam. Asking God what He wanted to show me, God told me that sometimes I was as stubborn as a donkey, but He would open my eyes and give me vision. And He would open my mouth and make me speak. The thought of God blessing me with more spiritual vision was awesome and exciting, but opening my mouth and making me speak was terrifying, and the thought brought dread to my heart.

Months passed. Then during my summer break from my job of teaching piano lessons, I felt a deep, subtle restlessness growing in me. I remember talking to God, saying, "Lord, you know that I am quite content in my life. You've been so good to me. I've served you all my life, even while I worked jobs and raised my family. Is there anything more you have for me to do? I am good if that's all; it's been a good life..." I was pouring out my heart to God but he didn't respond. I pondered those thoughts for days. Even my family noticed I was zoned out when they talked to me. I was visibly present, yet mentally distant.

A few weeks later, in August, I was flipping channels on TV and started listening to a Bible teacher speaking on Joshua 1:3-9 which was when God was commissioning Joshua to lead Israel after Moses died. As the teacher spoke, I was supernaturally spellbound.

Through every word, I was hearing God directly commissioning me. He said, "I will give you every place where you set your foot, as I promised Moses...No one will be able to stand up against you all the days of your life. As I was with Moses, so I will be with you; I will never leave you nor forsake you. Be strong and courageous, because you will lead my people. Be strong and very courageous. Be careful to obey all the law...do not turn from it to the right or to the left, that you may be successful wherever you go. Do not let this Book of the Law depart from your mouth; meditate on it day and night, so that you may be careful to do everything written in it. Then you will be prosperous and successful. Have I not commanded you? Be strong and courageous. Do not be terrified; do not be discouraged, for the LORD your God will be with you wherever you go."

The echoing command to be strong and courageous gave me goose bumps. I trusted God, but I was so painfully shy and fearful of having to speak in front of people that I was filled with anxiety. Sharing my thoughts with friends at Bible study would bring me to nervous tears. A few times at prayer meeting, I actually told people not to look at me while I shared what God had put on my heart to speak.

The whole ramification of what that passage in Joshua spoke to me, literally made me feel sick. "As I was with Moses, so I will be with you...because you will lead my people." Despite my terrible sense of dread about the future, there was a stirring in my spirit that is hard to describe. It was like an elation of intrigue, of mystery, of an adventure book unfolding, taunting me to sneak a glimpse at the next page. It was daring me to leap forward and engage with the plot of the story.

My journal of God moments was the key that brought me great understanding and comfort a month later, in September, when He gave me the vision for Hope House Ministries of Adonai. At that time, my emotions were stunned, and I basically walked through several days of being in shock and in denial that God really wanted me to lead a ministry.

What in the world was God thinking! I was a quiet, content, middle-aged lady, a wife, a mom, a grandmother, and I had a flourishing business that I loved. I had no dreams or inclination toward starting a ministry, so I told the Lord names of people who were perfect, full of energy and who would be thrilled to do it. But gently God urged me to read my journal. He quieted my fears and reminded me that all those days of my life were written for me when I was created. Psalms 139:16 "...all the days ordained for me were written in your book before one of them came to be."

For most of my life, I thought I was writing my story by myself. But God was making it perfectly clear that He was the Author. It was not randomly written by me or by chance, but by divine appointment. Ephesians 1:11-12 says that "In Him we were also chosen, having been predestined according to the plan of Him who works out everything in conformity with the purpose of His will, in order that we, who were the first to put our hope in Christ, might be for the praise of His glory."

My destiny, according to God's will and purpose, was that I would find my hope and salvation in Jesus Christ. That redeemed life story would bring Him praise and glory. Not only was God speaking into my destiny but into the destiny of Hope House Ministries as He revealed to me that "Millions will come through the House of Adonai, International."

As the puzzle pieces of God's revelation for my life and for Hope House Ministries continue to be carefully assembled, I have been finding myself often in His presence. My spirit longs to be with Him, listening to His voice. Many times, I have remained quiet about the things my Father has shared with me. But other times I know that I am to speak, remembering that "The Sovereign LORD has given me an instructed tongue, to know the word that sustains the weary." God speaks His Word through me to bring healing to those who are hurting and hope to those who are lost. They are touched and saved by the power of His Holy Spirit. Word of God, speak!

LET'S TALK ~ GOD'S HEART FOR YOU

God's Word speaks spiritual life into us. It's what our soul longs for. Psalm 130:5 "I wait for the LORD, my whole being (soul) waits, and in his word, I put my hope." When you read the Bible, it should bring peace, joy, conviction, understanding, and minister to your soul. Scripture should touch your daily life and bring insight to the situations you are working through. Some verses should speak to you in such a way that they help you to discern between God's truth and a deceitful version of truth.

Some verses will encourage and challenge you. The Word of God should sound like His voice speaking directly to you. If it doesn't, there is definitely a break in the connection. There's a problem somewhere.

The Bible was birthed by the Spirit of God. Man was the hand that wrote what was inspired by the Holy Spirit to be recorded. Sometimes the disconnect that people experience when reading the Scripture comes because they had a water birth, but not a Spirit birth. Flesh understands things of the flesh, but only spirit can fully understand things of the Spirit. Often there are wonderful folks who believe that they are Christians and are in right-standing with God because they attend a church and take communion. But they don't understand that they need more than participation. They need to be born again of the Spirit.

Jesus told Nicodemus about being born again. "...no one can enter the kingdom of God unless they are born of water and the Spirit. Flesh gives birth to flesh, but the Spirit gives birth to spirit" John 3:5-6. Jesus also said, "I am the way and the truth and the life. No one comes to the Father except through me" John 14:6. It is only through personally accepting Christ as your Savior that you can be filled with the Holy Spirit and have an eternal life with God.

Ephesians 1:13(NLV) "...And when you believed in Christ, He identified you as His own by giving you the Holy Spirit, whom He promised long ago." That is the spiritual birth that Jesus talked about with Nicodemus. It is the only sure way that you can access God and come into His Presence. The Holy Spirit, living within us, teaches and gives us revelation. It's through the Holy Spirit that reading the Bible comes alive in our hearts. It's by the Spirit that we can hear when God speaks to us in the Scripture, in prayer and in other ways. The Spirit brings understanding and Godly wisdom.

Isaiah 50:4 "The Sovereign LORD has given me a well-instructed tongue, to know the word that sustains the weary. He wakens me morning by morning, wakens my ear to listen like one being instructed." It's God's heart that you would be tuned into His voice each morning as you awaken to a new day–eager to be instructed so you can understand the word that ministers to your soul and to those who are weary. Having God's insight to your life puzzle, which often seems to be randomly scattered on a table, will fill you with the ability to connect pieces. It's a great reason to commit to journaling everything God is speaking and showing you, at least for a season. And it will set your life on the right path.

Proverbs 3:5-6 "Trust in the LORD with all your heart and lean not on your own understanding; in all your ways submit to him, and he will make your paths straight." When you trust in the Lord with all your heart and are fully submitted, then you are more prepared when He commissions you. God will keep your path straight so you don't stumble along the way that He has planned for you to go.

Joshua 1:3,5-9 (Passage in the story)

When God commissioned Joshua, He told him to 'be strong and courageous.' This passage applies to you and whatever purpose God has ordained for your life. You may be in a season of preparation. All of your puzzle pieces may not have been laid out on the table...yet. Maybe only a few clues have been connected, but not enough clues to give you a clear direction of what lies ahead. Even so, be ready! Trust in God and not in your own understanding. As

He opens doors and opportunities come, remember, you are to walk boldly. When it happens, don't be faint-hearted, God is with you and has taken hold of your right hand. Walk in obedience. Don't dread or be fearful of what God may ask you to do. He will be faithful to equip you each step of the way, just as you need it.

Always anticipate the thrill in every wondrous adventure you take with God. Even as I grow older and have physically slowed down a little, nothing can ever compare to the joy and excitement that comes to my heart when I feel the move of God in my spirit. Live your life full of hope each day, believing that God still holds more unseen puzzle pieces in His hand for you. My picture isn't quite complete, neither is yours—if you're still alive and breathing. It would be devastating if He withheld any pieces from our finished work. So pray this with me... 'Father, awaken my ear to listen, teach me morning by morning... Word of God, Speak. Amen.'

Reflection: Have you been listening for God's voice to speak to your heart?

Meditation music: Word of God, Speak or Take Time to be Holy

Maintenance

When it comes to car maintenance, my husband has always taken full responsibility for it. Last month, he noticed that my front tires were bald and too dangerous to drive on any longer. His work schedule was very hectic, so he told me that I needed to call the tire center for an appointment and take it there myself. I agreed to do it, since otherwise I would have been stranded at home indefinitely.

The serviceman told me to bring the car in right away. He said that they could put the new tires on, but I would have to wait a couple days before they could schedule an alignment. While the tires were being changed, I sat impatiently thinking about all the things that I could be doing if I wasn't stuck there...doing my husband's job! When the car was finished, I made an appointment for the alignment. They told me to plan on waiting there a couple of hours for that work to be done.

For the next two days, when I thought of the upcoming appointment and the chunk of wasted time sitting in the waiting room, I dreaded it. That morning, as I was leaving the house to go to the tire center, I remembered seeing some benches outside the door of the building. I grabbed a devotional book off of the shelf that I could read while I waited, but about a mile down the road, the Lord nudged me to turn around and return home to get my Bible and journal instead.

Soon I was sitting on a bench in the sunshine, spreading out my books. It was beautiful weather. A few others had the same idea, except they were sitting on their bench talking and laughing. "How am I supposed to concentrate on you, Lord, with that distraction!" As I opened up my Bible, the wind suddenly picked up, and soon there was a racket above me that was so loud that even the nearby traffic sound was blocked out. The maintenance men had strung ropes of triangle-shaped colored plastic flags that stretched from their business sign to the front of the building. The flapping noise was annoying at first, but as I continued to read, it began to muffle the background noise.

Time went by quickly. Hours later, the service manager had to bump my arm before I realized that he was standing beside me trying to get my attention. The car was finished, but I wasn't. I felt disappointed to leave the special place that God had provided. God's provision.

Later, while working at my desk at home, my thoughts kept returning to my afternoon on the bench. How reluctant I had been to do the car task, yet how faithful God was to be there when I went expecting and prepared with my Bible and journal. I thanked the Lord for that special time, and He responded by saying, "The road that I am calling you to follow doesn't leave room for unalignment. There is to be no pulling to the left or to the right. Be aware of any tugging, and don't adjust your driving to accommodate for it. Immediately go for rotation and balance. There is not to be a wearing away of the tires. They will need to remain deep-treaded, clearly defined, full of grip, and able to maintain any course or condition set before them."

As I wrote what He was speaking to my heart, familiar verses confirmed truth in those words. In Matthew 7:13-14, Jesus spoke of the narrow road that leads to life. The road God calls us to follow isn't broad. Unalignment could easily throw us into a ditch. "There is to be no pulling to the left or the right." Sometimes I have haphazardly veered off and taken a scenic route, like on days when I have skipped my devotion time to go shopping early or to get an extra hour of sleep. Even though I have good intentions of doing it later, too often I encounter a series of detours that keep me from it.

Deuteronomy 5:32 tells us, "So be careful to do what the Lord your God has commanded you; do not turn aside to the right or to the left." For example, God has specifically shown me 7:00 A.M. for devotions. I see those numbers clearly every time I think or hear the word devotions. Any wavering on the personal guidelines that God has set before me is a pulling to the left or the right.

"Be aware of any tugging, and don't adjust your driving to accommodate for it." In the Old Testament, Israel often fell into sin a little tug at a time, until their disobedient lives broke the heart of God. Many times, His anger against them was overwhelming. But instead of his intended destruction, He responded with tough love. God's mercy.

In Jeremiah 31, God promised Israel restoration. He had removed his protection and allowed the Babylonians to take them into captivity for seventy years. It was a time period of intense maintenance for Israel in re-establishing relationship and alignment with God. He drastically rotated their lives to bring about his desired balance. God's alignment.

Jeremiah 31:21 says, "Set up road signs; put up guideposts. Take note of the highway, the road that you take. Return, O Virgin Israel, return to your towns." It was important for their spiritual well-being to remember where they had been and the difficult road they had traveled because of their bad choices. The same holds true for us. When we feel inclined to take a scenic route, we need to recall our past "dead ends." All diversions that lead us away from the main road are sin. We need to quickly post the sign "Closed" across those options.

Regularly scheduled maintenance time with God and seeking to utilize all of the often- wasted moments in our day will give us endurance for the journey. It enables our spiritual tires to remain deep-treaded and clearly defined, full of grip and able to maintain any course and condition set before us.

As God instructed His returning people, who but God would embrace and endear them to His heart and call them "O Virgin Israel?" What incomprehensible grace He extended to them and extends to us, knowing our past, yet seeing us as unblemished and pure. Colossians 1:22 says "But now He (God) has reconciled you by Christ's physical body through death to present you as holy in His sight, without blemish and free from accusation." God lovingly calls His people back home, forgiving and restoring us despite our unworthiness. What unmerited favor! God's grace.

LET'S TALK ~ GOD'S HEART FOR YOU

MAINTENANCE: It keeps our cars running, our homes pleasantly clean, our bodies healthy and our souls aligned with God. When our cars need fixed, we repair them. When our homes get messy, we clean. When our bodies get sick, we take medicine. But when our souls become troubled, we have a tendency to ignore the signs of discontentment, disappointment, or whatever is disturbing the peace deep within us. We all have familiar avoidance tactics that take over to hide the problem. Some people shop, hang out with friends, spend time with social media, or watch Hallmark movies, like I do. For a while, it may divert our attention, but it doesn't fix us.

GOD'S PROVISION: When you become a Christian, you belong to God. You are His child and He promised to provide for you. The Lord cares about your family, your job, your health, and everything that happens to you. He knows what you need physically and spiritually. If your soul is troubled or you don't sense God's deep peace, seek the Lord through prayer and His Word. He will provide a 'quiet' place to meet with you, even in the midst of chaos or noise. He provides restoration for our souls. Psalm 51:10-12 says, "Create in me a pure heart, O God, and renew a steadfast spirit within me. Do not cast me from your presence or take your Holy Spirit from me. Restore to me the joy of your salvation and grant me a willing spirit, to sustain me."

GOD'S MERCY: No matter if we mess up over and over, God never gives up on us. When we repent of our sinful waywardness, He forgives us time after time, although we don't deserve it. Because of our Father's great love for us, He wipes the slate clean and gives us a fresh new start. Lamentations 3:22-23 (HCSB) tells us, "Because of the Lord's faithful love we do not perish, for His mercies never end, they are new every morning; great is Your faithfulness!"

GOD'S ALIGNMENT: When we carelessly veer off to the left or to the right, He is eager to set us back on track. He is faithful to pick us up, dust us off, and give us a push in the right direction. God's desire is to bless you with all the benefits that He provided for you through His plan of salvation. Once you have received Christ as your Savior, you are redeemed. The blood of Jesus, which brought you redemption, continues to atone for your sins and mistakes. The Holy Spirit's sanctifying work aligns your will to God's will. 2 Thessalonians 2:13 says, "But we ought always to thank God for you, brothers and sisters loved by the Lord, because God chose you as first-fruits [meaning from the beginning] to be saved through the sanctifying work of the Spirit and through belief in the truth."

GOD'S GRACE: This is a concept that defies our ability to comprehend it, just as we cannot fathom the depth of God's love. Grace is God's unmerited favor, blessing, and kindness. Grace is God choosing to bless us rather than curse us as our sin deserves. Grace is too extravagant for us to earn. We are told in Ephesians 2:8-10 "For it is by grace you have been saved, through faith—and this is not from yourselves, it is the gift of God—not by works, so that no one can boast. For we are God's handiwork, created in Christ Jesus to do good works, which God prepared in advance for us to do."

Grace is God giving the greatest treasure to the least deserving– which is every one of us. Accept His gift today and receive His Holy Spirit, who will begin transforming you through daily maintenance and careful alignment. You will be on the right road...the one that God has prepared for you to travel on the journey He has mapped out for you. Enjoy your trip!

Reflection: Is my life in alignment with God's direction, or have I veered off to the left or the right?

Meditation music: Reckless Love or The Ninety and Nine

12.

Jesus loves me this I know

YES! YES!

Jesus loves me   Jesus loves me

righteousness

The Song in my Heart

Childhood diseases are a part of everyone's life. We don't spend much time reminiscing about them because they aren't among our favorite memories. But one that was unforgettable for me was the time I had poison ivy, chicken pox, and measles all at the same time. I lived with five brothers and two sisters and must have been exposed to many germs. What I remember about that experience is mostly from what my mom has told me. She said while I was upstairs in bed, very sick, she could hear me constantly singing all the little Sunday School songs that I had learned.

> "Jesus loves me this I know; For the Bible tells me so.
> Little ones to Him belong; They are weak but He
> is strong."

So much of who we are has its roots in our childhood. Even at an early age, the songs about Jesus were not just catchy tunes to me. I truly loved Jesus because He loved me. He was the song in my heart. It was as simple as that, no question about it.

As I grew older, I never lost my love for Jesus and Christian music. If I wasn't singing, I was humming. Always, there was a song playing through in my heart. It wasn't unusual for me to wake during the night or in the morning and be in the middle of a song. Some people might raise their eyebrows and think that is pretty strange. But not me, I thought that was normal for everyone to have music playing in their head.

During this past summer, one night at Bible study we had gathered into a circle to pray. As I walked over to join in, a couple lines from a song kept going through my mind. I felt the Lord urging me to sing it out loud. Being shy, I didn't give in. All through the prayer time, the Lord kept pushing me. So finally, I spoke up and said "For some reason, God wants me to sing a couple lines of a song. Close your eyes and don't look at me." They chuckled and I began singing "Put on the garment of praise over the spirit of heaviness. Let the oil of gladness flow down from His throne." I sang it twice. When I finished, I heard people whispering "thank you Jesus" as we closed our prayer time.

The next week at church, my husband had the opportunity to present the message, so he shared his testimony. His story was that of a man who knew the Lord in his childhood but had slowly walked away. He told about his life that had been devastated by what had become the love of his life, alcohol. He went into detail, telling some of the hardships that he put his family through for many years.

Finally, the destructive cycle of addiction was broken when he admitted himself into a rehab unit. There he experienced a miracle of grace that changed his life forever. God spoke to his heart and began to transform his thoughts and mindset. The Lord healed his body that had been ravaged by abuse. Then my husband shared how God has been continuing that mighty work in his life, restoring and filling him with hope and plans for the future.

As my husband was preparing this message earlier in the week, it stirred up old memories. Normally, I purposely avoid reliving that time in my life. Even after many years, painful thoughts from the past can be troubling. God has healed our relationship, but some-times an unresolved issue stirs up emotions. Unless you have lived in a household with someone who has a long-term addiction, you have no clue of the toll it takes. You may have some understanding, but like anything that is devastating, you can't fully understand how it feels unless you have experienced it.

Late Sunday night, my Mother-in-law called me. She had come to our church to hear her son preach. Emotionally she said, "I'm so sorry for what my son put you through. I never knew it was so bad. You are a strong woman." I replied, "It's okay, Mom; God brought us through it. I was really weak, but God was my strength." I've always held tightly onto 2 Corinthians 12:9 which reads: "And he (God) said unto me, 'My grace is sufficient for thee: My strength is made perfect in weakness.'" I have known all my life where my strength is rooted.

For two weeks, the song that God had made me sing out at Bible study, kept going through my heart. Finally, when I was reading my Bible, I decided to see where that passage was found. It comes from Isaiah 61:3 "And provide for those who grieve in Zion to bestow on them a crown of beauty instead of ashes, the oil of gladness instead of mourning, and a garment of praise instead of a spirit of despair. They will be called oaks of righteousness, a planting of the Lord for the display of his splendor."

When I read this, I knew that God was showing me his fulfilled promise in my life. From a young age he had planted a love in my heart for him. I've loved praising him. It's as much a part of me as my hand. He knew that many times my life would be difficult. God showed me in that passage that because I daily put on a "garment of praise," He had poured his "oil of gladness" over me. An oil is not easily wiped away. Its residue remains until soaped off. Even then, some of it has already penetrated into the pores. During the worst of times, there was a deep-seated joy and peace that nothing could remove or rub away.

There were times that I grieved for my marriage. I cried out to my Father to touch my husband and restore our marriage. It didn't happen in my timing, but in God's. He has "bestowed upon it a crown of beauty instead of ashes." What could have been destroyed into ashes, He has crowned with his beauty. We've never been happier.

Many times, people have said to me that I was so strong. I'm not, and I wasn't then. But what they saw was that "oak of righteousness." The oak was the strength of the Lord surrounding me as I stood in Christ's righteousness. For I was "a planting of the Lord for the display of His splendor." The Lord knew where he had planted me and knew his purposes.

The circumstances of our lives are no surprise to him. Our Father provides all that we need to bring us through those hard times. As we cling to the Word of God, spend time in prayer, and lift up our praises to him, He hears us and is faithful. He pours his oil over us to sustain us with a joy and peace that could only be found in Him. May God be glorified in our lives, no matter what we are going through. For me, He will always be the song in my heart.

"Yes, Jesus loves me; Yes, Jesus loves me.
Yes, Jesus loves me; The Bible tells me so."

LET'S TALK ~ GOD'S HEART FOR YOU

We lead a church service at a nearby nursing home. When we sing Jesus Loves Me, it's amazing to see how many of the patients, who have Alzheimer's or dementia, suddenly begin to sing along. They remember the words. It's like God's love song was embedded in their spirit. They are weak, but He is strong.

What song has God put in your heart? Even a simple song like Jesus Loves Me can carry you through life's enduring troubles and hardships. Learning that song as a little girl, I knew that I would never be separated from Jesus's love because the Bible told me so. Not too long ago, my daughter Jennifer, and family went through a devastating loss that brought great heartbreak. As life kept moving them forward, a dark, eerie fog of oppression threatened to keep my daughter in a state of woundedness. But God...He put a song in her heart. Like a lullaby to her soul, the melody was a reminder that she was loved by her Father, and she truly only needed Him. Soon her heart began to sing the words,

'I just want You.' Only the Lord could restore the brokenness she felt. When her heart, mind, and soul became fully in-tune with God's compassion, my daughter was able to let go of the past and focus on the horizon of good things that God has planned for her tomorrows. She has become "a planting of the Lord for the display of His splendor." God once again brought beauty from ashes. No wonder throughout Scripture, we are constantly told about God's all-encompassing love for us.

Romans 8:38 (NLT) "And I am convinced that nothing can ever separate us from God's love. Neither death nor life, neither angels nor demons, neither our fears for today nor our worries about tomorrow—not even the powers of hell can separate us from God's love."

Nothing can separate you from the love of God. Sin is a wall that can block your relationship with God, but He still loves you. You might have separated yourself from Him because of guilt and shame, but God has not separated Himself from you. He might hate what you are doing wrong and the bad choices you've made, but in His love, He is always ready to forgive, if you ask. God's not mad at you, He's mad about you!

Isaiah 61:3 "And provide for those who grieve in Zion to bestow on them a crown of beauty instead of ashes, the oil of gladness instead of mourning, and a garment of praise instead of a spirit of despair. They will be called oaks of righteousness, a planting of the Lord for the display of his splendor."

This passage was written by Isaiah for the future, when the nation of Israel would face seventy years of captivity in Babylon for their rebellious behavior against God. During those years, they would repent and seek God. These Scriptures were written to encourage and give them hope. They were to 'put on a garment of praise'—symbolically. Praising God would break the spirit of despair and heaviness. When their focus was on Him, transformation and breakthrough would be possible. Even if they were not released from bondage physically, in their hearts and spirit they would experience freedom and hope. God had poured out the oil of gladness from His throne. He would be their strength, and their captors would see the glory of God in them.

Whatever you have been through in this life, whatever has caused you to grieve or mourn, God can bring forth a transformation of beauty from ashes. Deep peace and joy come from salvation—surrendering your life to Him. The more you begin to look through the glass of God's perspective, rather than your own, the more you will see God's presence in everything concerning your life.

Ask God to fill you with His song and Scriptures to revive your spirit. Let them be embedded into your soul. God's heart for you is to draw you to a place of freedom from whatever troubles you. Through His loving transformation, you will become an oak of Christ's righteousness. You will be a planting of the Lord. He will place you in a position to bring a sacred harvest. You were designed to be a display of His splendor so that people would experience your Father's glory. You are chosen by God to wear a crown of beauty instead of ashes. Rejoice as you wait upon the Lord. In His timing, you will see the faithfulness of God.

Reflection: You were created to be a display of God's splendor. His transformation power can touch you and your circumstances to bring beauty from ashes.

Meditation music: 10,000 Reasons or In My Heart There Rings a Melody

13.

Cord of Fear

$\mathcal{A}$ s Christians, we are all called to be prayer warriors. That is one of the most important aspects of our walk with Christ. Not only do we have obvious needs to lift before our Father, but we are surrounded by constant, unseen spiritual battles...invisible, yet real.

There has been a reoccurring dream in my life, ongoing for many years. It takes place in a house. The inside of the home is beautiful with each room overlooking another room. Usually the dream ends after I walk up to the bedroom loft and stand at the railing looking down over the dining room. One particular time, some children followed me up the steps to that room. In the hallway, they noticed another steep, old wooden staircase leading to another level. Curiosity sparked, and soon we were creeping slowly, single file, up that creaky, narrow passageway.

With the children in tow, I went first so that I could push the attic door open. Soon the door was lifted up and out of the way. I took another step higher. My eyes, which were even with the floor, made contact with a sight that ingrained an image in my mind that I will never forget. There was a woman lying on the floor fully dressed with her shoes on, but she was tied down with ropes and unable to move. There were ropes around her ankles, legs, and wrists. And something covered her mouth to keep her voice

75

from being heard. The horrific scene took my breath away. I was stunned. Immediately, I awakened and began to pray for this lady and other women who were being held in bondage.

Some people are called by God into the ministry of intercessory prayer. He bestows that unique spiritual gift which enables them to remain focused on prayer needs for great periods of time. The burden on my heart for those captive women remained. And I began to wonder if the Lord was leading me in that direction. Day after day, I asked the Lord to protect, comfort, and be with them. I pleaded for Him to help them escape and deliver them out of bondage.

During this time period, our Bible study group began to discuss dreams and the possible significance of some of them. I shared this particular one with them. Someone suggested that since a house is sometimes symbolic of our self, perhaps the woman in the attic was me. That idea was quickly denied; I didn't want that to be the case. Six months later, while diligently lifting up that lady in prayer, the Lord revealed to me that I was indeed that woman. He heard my plea for help. He told me that He was cutting away my ropes of bondage.

Psalm 119:61 states that "Though the wicked bind me with ropes, I will not forget your law." It is the enemy's scheme to tie braided cords over multiple areas in our lives. We can be in an intimate relationship with Christ and not recognize all of the places that Satan has compromised in us. It is only through God's revelation that we are able to see them. Slowly, over time, the cords can build up, twisting one to another until it resembles a rope... sometimes growing as thick as a bull rope.

One weekend, shortly after God had revealed this truth to me, I attended an Inner Healing seminar. The Lord set about working on one of the thickest ropes that held me down...fear. Fear encompasses a bevy of emotions. It can be disabling even for a Christian who has found spiritual freedom through Christ. While fear can be cleverly suppressed and kept hidden from other people, we who are dealing with it suffer deeply with its sinister flare-ups.

During this conference, we were encouraged to pray for God to reveal a troubled area that He wanted to help us work on. Mine was fear and intimidation. Then we were given some time to seek

God and to ask Him to show us where the root of that problem began. Within a few minutes, I saw myself as a five-year-old first grader. My Dad had taken me to the dentist. Afterwards, when he dropped me off at school, he watched me put my hand on the door handle; then he drove away. When I pushed the handle down, it was locked. I stood there awhile looking through the door window, watching for someone to see me. But no one came to help.

I didn't know what to do, so I walked around the building until I found another door. I climbed up some cement steps to reach it. But it was locked and wouldn't budge either. Again, I watched through the window, knocked, and waited for help, but no one came. Trembling with fear, tears began rolling down my cheeks as I set off to find another way to get inside. Finally, I found a door by the office that was unlocked. Once inside, I stood a few minutes looking down the hallways, wondering which direction to go. I was too afraid to go into the office to ask for help. I thought that I would be in trouble for being so late. Finally, I wandered through the halls until I found my classroom.

That traumatic experience opened an emotional pathway for Satan to attach a "cord of fear." Once fear took hold, it wasn't going to let go of me without a fight. Fear continued to build up over the years, one strand at a time, braiding and attaching itself to the core of my soul.

Understanding this concept, I know why the Lord had said that He was beginning to cut away the ropes. It's a process that can require a lot of spiritual work. I had lived with my fear for so long that I believed it was just a part of my personality. I had become comfortable in the sense that I had learned to alleviate the hard edge of my fear by manipulating each unnerving situation I faced. I had learned to be quietly controlling of people to protect myself.

Then the teacher leading the healing session instructed us to bow our heads again in prayer. We were told to look again at the traumatic scene until we were able to see where Jesus was in the picture. In Hebrews 13:5, God has said, "Never will I leave you; never will I forsake you." The Lord showed me that He was there all the time following that little girl, holding His arms out ready to catch her if she fell. Jesus watched out for me from behind, yet his eyes were also scanning in front of me. It reminded me of the passage in Psalm 139:5 (BSB), "You hem me in behind and before; You have laid your hand upon me." It was a healing moment that began an ongoing process of seeing Jesus in other situations that have caused fear in my life.

Fighting a spiritual, unseen battle requires the discipline of a well-trained warrior who spends much time in prayer. 2 Corinthians 10:3-5 tells us, "For though we live in the world, we do not wage war as the world does. The weapons we fight with are not the weapons of the world. On the contrary, they have (God's) divine power to demolish strongholds. We demolish arguments and every pretension that sets itself up against the knowledge of God, and we take captive every thought to make it obedient to Christ."

Because I had been so tangled up in cords of lies from Satan, every thought that provoked any measure of fear in me needed to be prayerfully submitted to Jesus Christ. He taught me to stand firm in the battle by the authority of the Holy Spirit that dwelled within me. Fighting the devil, by speaking the Word of God to cast out fear, was a double-edged sword. That weapon began to gradually cut the ropes loose to free me. "It is for freedom that Christ has set us free. Stand firm, then, and do not let yourselves be burdened by a yoke of slavery." Galatians 5:1. Fear was my yoke of slavery.

Breaking free from my years of spiritual bondage required a lot of studying. Finding specific scriptures that contradicted the stronghold shredded the fibers of the rope. The cord of fear had tied my hands, keeping me from reaching out to others and my feet from stepping out in faith. My voice had been muffled by a stranglehold of intimidation. I was afraid of being ridiculed, belittled, or sounding foolish if I talked in front of people. For too many years, fear silenced me from sharing my testimony of God's love and salvation.

"Out of my distress I called on the LORD; the LORD answered me and set me free." Psalm 118:5 (ESV) No longer will fear bind or restrain me from whatever God calls me to do or say. Fear will no longer dictate boundaries or voice restrictions over my life or ministry. "And the God of all grace, who called you to His eternal glory in Christ...will Himself restore you and make you strong, firm, and steadfast" 1 Peter 5:10. Wrapped safely in grace, I am fearless and courageous. God has brought me home to His place of freedom.

LET'S TALK ~ GOD'S HEART FOR YOU

God's heart is that you would not suffer from any type of spiritual stronghold that alters the life He planned for you. God created you perfect and beautiful. Yet sometimes a trait or emotion that has always been normal can become a vulnerable area. Only God knows how the enemy can detect where he might have a chance to harm you.

2 Timothy 1:7 (NKJV) tells us, "For God has not given us a spirit of fear, but of power and of love and of a sound mind." God did not give you a 'spirit of fear' although fear is one of the emotions that every living creature was given. Basically, it was given for protection. When you are in danger, a flash of fear alerts you to be cautious. The problem comes when fear becomes unbalanced. Escalated fear can become an ugly beast of oppression when the enemy is behind it. It can develop into a yoke of slavery. Fear can be defined as a stronghold when it starts to consume your thoughts and direct your actions.

God gave you a spirit of power, love, and a sound mind so that you can be a mighty warrior who can successfully fight the unseen battles stirred up by Satan. You are to be courageous. And you need to understand the offensive-defensive potential of your armor. Your helmet of salvation, breastplate of righteousness, shield of faith, sword of the Spirit, and shoes of peace together, along with prayer and thanksgiving, will always bring victory. Study about it in Ephesians 6.

Isaiah 54:17 (NAS) assures us that "No weapon that is formed against you will prosper; and every tongue that accuses you in judgment you will condemn. This is the heritage of the servants of the Lord, And, their vindication is from Me," declares the Lord.

John 8:44 also warns us about Satan. It says, "...for he is a liar, and the father of lies." You need to know that Satan's tongue tries to accuse and tear you down as he attempts to get you to believe his lies are the truth. The devil is a professional liar, who intentionally bombards your mind. with fearful thoughts. He will do everything he can to paralyze you to keep you from walking out God's plan. He wants to kill, steal and destroy you. Therefore, you must stand firm on God's truth and cast fear into the fire to be destroyed. One of the most effective things that I did, after I came home from that Inner Healing conference was to buy index cards that were spiral bound. I spent time looking up every verse in the Bible that talked about fear. Then I picked out helpful verses that pertained to my fear and wrote one on each card. When I felt fear rising up inside of me, I was able to quickly grab a verse, and then I could speak it out loud to let the enemy know that I was calling on the power of God. As time went on, I memorized some of the verses so I was always equipped to go to battle against the liar.

Fear may not be a problem for you. Maybe while you were reading this, God brought to mind something else in your life that is troubling and has escalated to become a controlling factor. It could be anything that holds you back from God's will and plan. It keeps you from reaching out to people, stepping out in faith, or sharing your testimony of God's love and salvation. Find verses which speak to whatever issue that you may struggle against. Then write the Scripture down so that you have it at your fingertips when you need a mighty weapon.

Anything that keeps you from being all that God created you to be could be an indication of a spiritual issue. Seek God's wisdom and revelation. Ask Him to reveal the root of the problem, and where it began. Keep praying until God shows you where He was during this situation or scenario. Know that God never leaves us nor forsakes us; you were not alone. Even if you weren't a Christian at the time, and no matter what happened, God was present. There are about a hundred Bible verses that speak about the omni-presence of God. "The eyes of the LORD are everywhere, keeping watch on the wicked and the good." Proverbs 15:3

Psalm 139:5 (BSB) says, "You hem me in behind and before; You have laid your hand upon me." God has been watching over you in the past and will be in the future. God's hand has been lovingly touching you. He wants to bring you healing, comfort, and peace.

Before God began cutting away the cord of fear in my life, I struggled with a lot of guilt from not doing the good things that He wanted me to do. There was a lady that I loved all my life who had been placed in a large three-story nursing home. I desperately wanted to go and visit her before she passed away. But fear of the unknown, becoming lost and not being able to find her room, kept me from going. Every time I drove past the building, I felt terribly guilty and ashamed of myself.

Shortly after that, God began breaking the stronghold in me. During the restoration process, He opened the door for Hope House Ministry to host a church service there once or twice a month. An important part of my breakthrough involved me trusting God enough to help me face one of the most fearful things in my past. Each time I went, it became a little less nerve racking than the time before. Finally, I began to look forward to going. God filled me with love for all the dear residents and workers there. Now I lead a Bible study there each week, along with the ongoing church services. We've been serving there for fifteen years.

It's rather amazing that God took one of my biggest fears and turned it around to be one of my biggest joys. Never underestimate the powerful love of God. His heart for you is that you would become spiritually awakened, filled with His Spirit, and prepared to experience everything that He has planned for you. God wants your heart to dwell with His. Surrender anything that has been hindering you or holding you back from living this life fully-alive in Christ Jesus. Dare to defy the devil's diversions. God will rejoice as He breaks whatever binds you and brings you home to a new life, His place of freedom.

Reflection: What is holding me back from living this life fully alive in Jesus Christ?

Meditation music: Place of Freedom or Because He Lives

14.

The Whirlwind

There's a chorus of a beautiful song about the faithfulness of God that keeps playing through my mind this morning. The lyrics of the verse come from Psalms 136:1, "Give thanks to the LORD, for he is good, His love endures forever." A similar verse can be found a few other places but I especially like the added dimension of Psalms 100:5, "For the LORD is good and his love endures forever; His faithfulness continues through all generations."

So often around the holidays, the pace of life picks up. We are filled with anticipation and excitement as we make plans to gather with family and friends to celebrate. Super Bowl games, weddings, and vacations are other occasions that can fit into that same category. Usually they involve extra shopping, phone calls, planning sessions and baking...all of which some of us enjoy as much as the event itself! When those times come, it's easy to get caught up in the whirlwind surrounding us. Just going with the flow of activities is usually fun and harmless, but not always. Sometimes it is wise to pull back and be still.

This past week, the pace of a new ministry that I am involved with seems to be accelerating. We are in the stages of building a strong organizational network and expanding our boundaries. Until now, the vision of the ministry has resided in our hearts and prayers. Except for a ladies' retreat, prayer ministry, and completed legal work, there hasn't been a physical aspect to this vision. Now there's a whirl of movement thrusting forward that reminds me of a roller coaster ride. For a long period of time, we have been taking a few small steps, waiting, and then going a couple more, like in the "cattle pens" before the main ride. Finally, after passing through the gate, we are now ready to find our seats and our position within the organization. Strapping in for the exhilarating adventure brings a nervous excitement, building up anticipation for the unfamiliar experience ahead.

When it comes to safety, we can't be overly cautious. Examining the strength of the belt that keeps us out of harm's way makes a lot of sense. Yesterday, amid the whirlwind, I felt compelled to yank and tug at what was fastening me into place. I knew it was time to pull myself away and find out who was powering the wind that was blowing around me. I thought and hoped it was God, but I had to be absolutely certain. Determined not to go any further until knew without a doubt, I asked God to make it clear. As I prayed, I felt an urge to go back through some of the past entries in my daily journal. Henry Blackaby, a well-known Christian teacher-speaker, was leading a seminar that I attended. He had talked about the importance of journaling. I still remember him saying words to this effect, that if we truly expect God to show up during our quiet time, why wouldn't we want to write down what He says. After all, He is God...so whatever God seems to be telling me, I write.

Searching throughout my books, there were several confirmations of the preparation timetable for this ministry. In my journaling, I found some long-forgotten words of God's encouragement that He had spoken to me, and other words of confirmation that came from some of my spiritual mentors. Over and over Scripture verses were highlighted and recorded on the pages. God made His faithfulness known to me through the instructions that were already printed there in advance. He knew this moment would come when I needed assurance. My Father knew that I would need to know without a doubt who was in control, and if there was danger. He planned for this day knowing my cowardly instincts would drive me to test the seat belt before the big ride.

A short time after I started writing this devotional, we went to the Spring Festival at a nearby church. The speaker's message was about seasons. It was based on the following passages in the Song of Songs 2:11-12 "See! The winter is past; the rains are over and gone. Flowers appear on the earth; the season of singing has come; the cooing of doves is heard in our land." There are obvious seasons in nature but the Bible shows that there are also seasons in our lives spiritually. When life seems to be at a standstill or in a period of dormancy, winter has settled on us. It's a time when we wait in hopefulness, looking for signs of spring, while abiding in Christ.

Isaiah 43:18-19 says "Forget the former things; do not dwell on the past. See, I am doing a new thing! Now it springs up; do you not perceive it? I am making a way in the desert and streams in the wasteland." Through Isaiah, the Lord spoke to Israel that it was time to forget about their years of slavery in Egypt and know that they had entered into a new season. Circumstances had changed as quickly as one day changes into another, one second after midnight. God urged the people to pay attention to the signs and recognize what he was doing. He wanted them to move forward, trusting Him, anticipating the miraculous journey to their new land.

The whirlwind I had experienced was the changing of season in our ministry and in my life. Winter was past and spring was bursting forth, with a thrust that caught me off guard. I didn't fully understand what was happening, so I instinctively jammed on the brakes with both feet...until I could find God in it.

You see, God isn't offended when we have questions about our circumstance and search for a glimpse of assurance. There is wisdom to be found in those moments as we examine the signs that He has posted for us. Even the prophet Jeremiah recognized a ray of hope, a sign, despite the turmoil that surrounded him, and spoke, "Yet this I call to mind and therefore I have hope: Because of the LORD's great love we are not consumed, for his compassions never fail. They are new every morning; great is your faithfulness.

I say to myself, 'The Lord is my portion; therefore, I will wait for him.'" Lamentations 3:21-22

The essence of God's enduring love is portrayed through His encompassing faithfulness over us. No matter in whatever season of life we find ourselves, there should be absolute peace in the knowledge that our Heavenly Father is in control. In times of deep searching, there is confirmation through resources God places at our fingertips such as the Bible, our journals, an inspirational book, or as we listen to a hauntingly beautiful worship song He plays in our heart. Knowing we are in His presence whether the wind is whirling or calm, we can trust our magnificent God to carry us in the current of His faithful love, witnessing generations of His faithfulness!

LET'S TALK ~ GOD'S HEART FOR YOU

Are you prepared for an unexpected whirlwind?

Are you ready to face a challenge that you feel unqualified to handle or a mountain that looks impossible to climb?

It's only a matter of time before everyone faces those situations, and most of the time it happens when we least expect it. That whirlwind was my experience years ago when God was establishing Hope House Ministry. It was a time when He was leading us into an unfamiliar territory. Personally, I felt untrained professionally for the job of leading the team to climb this impossible mountain that loomed before us.

Psalm 37:23 (NLT) "The Lord directs the steps of the godly. He delights in every detail of their lives." According to this verse, God was going to be faithful in directing my steps. My job was not to direct where this ministry team would go or how they would accomplish the task. My part was to put every area of my life under the righteousness of Christ, and be humbly submissive when the Holy Spirit was working hard to transform and adjust my attitudes, actions, and habits. God then led us to step out in faith. The faithfulness of God is not dependent upon our own faithfulness. And when we slip into that kind of thinking, even for a short time, usually it's a semi-victory for the enemy to get his way with us. A month ago, I was doing well at finishing up some of my stories that still needed the wrap-up section added. Then I told a friend that I should be able to submit this book for publishing the next month because I only had two more stories to finish, and one more full story to write. I truly believe that Satan heard me speak those words, and then he set about to do everything in his power to stop me.

Meanwhile, it's been a month since I have written one word due to a whirlwind of busyness, distractions, and an overwhelming sense of inadequacy to complete the job. At night, I have been dreaming...actually it's been more like a nightmare...that the book was a complete flop, and not worth finishing. I have been feeling guilty that I have not been very faithful in spending enough time with my Father lately. I have felt that ideas and inspiration have not come because I have failed God. I was falling into a rut; my mind was starting to dig a path in my brain that led away from God's plan. But then I shared my concern, and nightmare, with my Bible Study group during prayer time. The Lord heard my plea for help.

Psalm 40:2 "He lifted me out of the slimy pit, out of the mud and mire; He set my feet on a rock and gave me a firm place to stand." God pulled me out the enemy's pit that was meant to pull me under like quicksand. He lifted my soul and set me on the rock of His faithful promise to me. God has been reminding me that He's the author; He told me to write the book. I didn't ask to do this thing; therefore, I am to stand on the fact that my Father will be faithful to fulfill His planned purpose for it.

This morning, I am trusting in Him to meet with me, here in this moment of truth. Remembering the faithfulness of the Lord, my feet have found a firm place to stand. Not only has the Lord given me a firm foundation at this present time, He has reminded me of His faithfulness through generations in my family. I was named after my Grandma Pearl, who died before I was born. She must have loved the Lord, because on the day that she passed away, she was laying in the living room, smiling constantly as she stared at a spot above the fireplace. Finally, one of the family asked her why she kept smiling and staring; she said, "Don't you see, Jesus is here." She had spiritual vision to see Jesus waiting there to take her home. God's faithfulness to be with her, and to comfort her in her dying hours, is a story that I'll never forget. Psalm 100:5 tells us that "His faithfulness continues through all generations."

God's heart for you is that you would know that His faithfulness throughout your family generations has preserved your family and your own life. Without God's generations of protection throughout time, you would not exist. No matter if you come from a godly family or one with an unsavory past, someone throughout time must have touched the heart of God for Him to value your life and bring you into being. When He created you, it was with great forethought and planned purpose. Perhaps you are the one in your family who will touch the heart of God, bringing His favor and blessing on your future generations.

No matter what is happening in your life today, or what you may be facing tomorrow, focus on the knowledge that you are loved by a faithful Father. He cares about every detail of your life. God will never expect you to live up to the measure of His own ability to be faithful. You will fail Him; you will fail yourself. He already knows you are capable of making whopping mistakes, especially when you get caught up in a whirlwind that is swirling beyond your control. At those moments, pull yourself back, and find out who is behind the wind that is blowing you around. Be still, pray, listen, and wait for God's peace to come. Trust Him to meet with you in your time of need, and you will experience the unfailing faithfulness of God.

Reflection: Open my spiritual eyes to see the depth of your faithfulness in my life and throughout the past generations of my family.

Meditation music: Forever or Great is Thy Faithfulness

15.

The Call of Summer

When I was a little girl, I can remember so clearly how anxiously I waited for summer to come. Even before I was old enough to go to school, I can remember loving summer so much that at night, I would lay out my clothes for morning. That way I could quickly slip into them and go outside as soon as I woke up. Summer called my heart, and nothing else mattered.

For me, the most exciting time during summer was our annual trip to Lake Erie. We would pack our clothes, a few sand toys, and our beach towels. And of course, my Mom would pack a large cooler and picnic basket full of food for the day. On the two-hour drive, I remember playing simple road games. Each team counted cows on their side of the road. If we passed a cemetery on my side of the road, my team had to bury our cows and start counting all over again. Of course, the other team had to do the same thing if the graveyard was on their side of the road. It kept our attention for a while; then we'd pull out the car bingo game.

But as we neared Erie, no longer did those games matter to me, because my heart was drawn away, and my eyes began to watch intently for the lake. For miles, every hill we drove over,

I remember holding my breath, anticipating my first glimpse of the light blue sky touching the deeper blue of the lake. My heart yearned for that moment of vision. The vocal fussing of my siblings sitting around me faded out, because my ears were already tuning in to the air waves of the lake's water. In my imaginings, I could already hear the sound of the waves rolling onto the shore, and I could already see myself frolicking in the water. Memories, stirred with anticipation, brought to life all that my young heart desired and longed for at that special moment in time.

A few decades later, my beloved summertime came again, bringing along with it an unexpected sense of anticipation. Coming out of a season of prayer, during which God was establishing Hope House Ministries spiritually and legally, a restlessness began stirring in my spirit. I couldn't quite put my finger on the problem and spent about a week feeling very edgy and antsy.

Finally, I talked to my husband about it, because I thought that I just needed to get away for a few days. My mind and heart had begun to fixate on seeing the ocean. Although I had never been there before, I was having daydreams about sitting on the sand dunes for hours, while watching huge, mighty waves rolling in from a far-off distance. I followed them with my eyes, and they seemed to increase in strength and power as they came crashing onto the shore. Each wave of the sea took my breath away, as I anticipated its ability to wash over the beach, shifting the sand and sometimes washing away debris. Other times the waves would leave deposits—treasures of seashells or seasoned driftwood that had been uniquely created over time. Some were beautifully smoothed as if they were hand-sanded by the 'old man of the sea.'

During those days of restlessness, God began to speak to me as I was reading in the book of Isaiah. Subtitled "A Call to Trust the Lord," verse 51:1 said, "Listen to me, you who pursue righteousness and who seek the LORD..." It was followed later by verse 7 that also began with "Listen to me." As I read further, God began speaking directly to my spirit, saying, "For I am the LORD your God, who stirs up the sea so that its waves roar— the LORD Almighty is his name." Isaiah 51:15.

Suddenly my yearning heart understood my daydreams and my sense of anticipation and restlessness. God was calling me to see and understand what He was about to do with Hope House. Figuratively speaking, my Father was calling me into deep waters—where I'd never been before. And I would behold His mysterious power as His waves would begin to roll over the lives of those who would come into Hope House ministry. In my daydreams, I sat on sand dunes watching as the relentless waves came crashing onto the shore. God was showing me that I would see Him stirring up the sea, sending His mighty waves to wash over people's lives. I would see Him cleansing them, then depositing His treasures in their lives, and changing them forever to be like uniquely polished driftwood, finished by His sovereign hand.

God was calling my heart to trust in whatever He was about to do through this new ministry. I was to come and walk upon the water like Peter, with my eyes focused on Jesus. Each step of faith would make me stronger, knowing His presence was with me.

The passage in Isaiah 51:16 continued with God saying, "I have put my words in your mouth and covered you with the shadow of my hand..." God promised that He would be with me and that I could trust Him to speak through me, while I remained protected and hidden by the shadow of His hand. God was about to activate the ministry, and He had given me confidence that He was mightier than my fears. Since that time—these past sixteen years of ministry, God has been faithful. His grace has been sufficient for me; His power has been made perfect in my weakness.

From time to time, a remnant of that 'little girl' still living deep inside of me begins to yearn for the delightful adventures of summer. I lay out my clothes and wait for morning. Once again, 'the call of summer' woos my heart. My Father starts stirring up my senses to long for another mighty wave of His power and glory, and I'm ready to go to the sea.

The sovereignty of God's grace abounds in my life, and I will forever seek to be in His Presence, for I am His and He is mine.

LET'S TALK ~ GOD'S HEART FOR YOU

If there was a chapter written about your life during this past season, what would the author use as a subtitle? What would you call it? Isaiah 51 is subtitled "A Call to Trust the Lord." It starts out calling for our attention; "Listen to me, you who pursue righteousness and who seek the LORD..." It is followed later by verse 7; "Listen to me." God is trying to make sure that we are focused on what He is about to say. He knows how short our attention span can be. Reading a few verses further, God declares, "For I am the LORD your God, who stirs up the sea so that its waves roar– the LORD Almighty is his name." Isaiah 51:15.

Now, apply God's word directly to your life and your heart's deepest longings. Whatever is happening in your life, whatever situation or circumstance that needs to change, is not beyond the ability of the LORD Almighty to touch with His transforming power. When we are in the middle of difficult storms raging in our circle of life, often we assume the devil is behind it all. We don't like to consider the fact that sometimes it is God who is stirring up the waves, not to drown us, but to see if we will trust Him.

Matthew 14:28-33 tells us the story of Peter, who found himself surrounded by wickedly huge, life-threatening waves. He was with the disciples on a boat, in the middle of the sea of Galilee, in a storm that was so powerful that it was impossible for them to row back to the shore. Meanwhile, Jesus had gone up a nearby mountainside to rest and pray. He was well aware of what was happening to His men. As a matter of fact, we can also believe that He knew exactly the moment when the disciples would be extremely anxious and so filled with fear that their faith would be shaken. At that moment, would the subtitle of their life be, 'A Call to Trust the Lord?'

Of the 12 men in the boat, only one had enough faith to trust the Lord. When Jesus came walking on the water to rescue them, they thought He was a ghost. "But Jesus immediately said to them, 'Take courage! It is I. Don't be afraid.' 'Lord, if it's you,' Peter replied, 'tell me to come to you on the water.' 'Come,' He said. Then Peter got down out of the boat, walked on the water and came toward Jesus." Matthew 14:27-29 Peter had the courage to step out in faith. He trusted Jesus enough to venture into the deep water to obey the call of the LORD. Of course, if you know the whole story, Peter only took a few steps, then he faltered and started to sink. But Jesus was there to rescue him. He reprimanded him on his lack of faith, but Peter learned an important lesson—trust God despite the human tendency to cave in to fear. Where fear reigns, faith is driven away. But where faith reigns, fear has no place to stand.

God's heart for you is that your faith would be steadfast so that you would be able to stand firm in difficult times. And when you hear the call of God telling you to 'Come' and to do the seemingly impossible, you will remember what Jesus said; "With man this is impossible, but with God all things are possible." Matthew 19:26 God's grace abounds when He calls you into the deepest waters—the place that you would be terrified to go without His presence. But trust Him; His hand will guide you. When you are surrendered to your Father's will, you will see the miraculous moving of the Holy Spirit working on your behalf and in the lives of those around you.

Are you feeling a restlessness in your soul? Is God stirring up something inside of you? Call upon His name and keep your eyes searching above the waves. Focus on Jesus' open arms and your soul will be embraced within a safe place. No matter what happens, you belong to the LORD Almighty who declares to you, "I have put my words in your mouth and covered you with the shadow of my hand..." Isaiah 51:16. God promises to give you the words to speak, with His authority, into every situation that comes into your life. And you are covered by the awesome shadow of His hand as the Holy Spirit guides you into the unknown. You may not know what the outcome will be, but God knows.

Morning is coming; lay out your clothes and be ready for a summer of God's mighty waves washing over your life. Be cleansed, and collect all the treasures that He has deposited for you to discover. Have child-like faith, and experience the wonders of God's glory. Be refreshed as you anticipate His marvelous plan unfolding for this new day. Enjoy every moment, as you frolic in the light of your Father's love, and may His Son forever shine on your soul!

Reflection: Is God calling your heart to come into deep waters with Him and experience something unexpected?

Meditation music: Shout to the Lord or Here I Am, Lord

16.

Ring of Fire

Ideally, for a Christian, life should be like a walk through a beautiful garden, strolling along with the Lord just like I can envision Adam and Eve doing before sin entered the scene. No worries, problems, or distractions could mar that perfect picture of friendship. Unfortunately, we don't live in Eden and God's kingdom hasn't come. Satan is still on the loose in this world and stirs up trouble in our lives. Yet, a believer can and should be experiencing that 'garden fellowship' with God each day, entering into that beautiful place through worship, prayer, and reading His Word.

There is another prominent garden in the Bible that is found in Matthew 26:36. Jesus took His disciples to the Garden of Gethsemane, and then He went off alone to pray and talk with His Father. We have all seen paintings of that lovely setting with Jesus kneeling and peacefully praying, His hands folded on a rock. Even as a child, that was a comforting picture for me. But I didn't truly understand what was actually happening to Christ in that garden. Years later, after studying the Scripture story, I realized that Jesus was in such agony that He was sweating drops of blood. Not only did my visual perception change, but at some point, Gethsemane took on an unexpected reality in my life.

God has been establishing a ministry in my life that has plenty of opportunities in which to serve. Offering myself to Him, I have set my mind and will to do anything He asks, obediently. But God... being God, knows that I have withheld one thing. Several months ago, as I studied Isaiah 62, I began to scribble pages of notes while thinking, "This is the scripture that God wants for the upcoming women's retreat." Having a driving urgency to continue to take notes and write how it could apply to the lives of women, I kept thinking, "Why am I doing this? I can't give these notes to a guest speaker and tell her that this is for her message."

Meanwhile, unable to stop the course I was on until I reached the end of the chapter, I began to get a nauseating feeling in the pit of my stomach. Slowly, I began to understand what God was up to and what was happening. Fighting against the dreadful thought, I realized that He was asking me to do that one and only thing that I had not offered Him. It was the one thing that I feared the most all my life...speaking in front of people.

Struggling in an emotional battle of wills—mine vs God's, I went for my morning shower, expecting to receive some refreshing revelation, but it didn't happen that way. Turning off the water, I leaned against the wall sobbing; my stomach was so knotted in turmoil, it reminded me of labor pains. I was feeling such agony that I stretched my hand toward heaven and pleaded, "Father, please let this cup pass from me, if it be your will!" How pathetic I must have looked to God! Then I heard His Voice gently say, "I'm *not* asking you to die on the cross." Hanging my head in shame and asking for forgiveness, I numbly submitted to His will. It brought me a weird feeling of being peacefully dazed, knowing my course was set. I knew that I would obediently follow God's will, not mine.

A few days later, while thinking about the retreat, I suddenly visualized a huge 'ring of fire', like those at a circus for the trained animals to jump through. It was obvious that the flames represented extreme fear. Every time I thought about speaking in front of the group of ladies, I could see myself stuttering and then collapsing on the floor from weak knees. Satan's plan was to fuel that fearsome flame of fire. But my merciful Father turned that whole threatening scenario around. He said that every time I pictured that burning 'ring of fire', I was to know that He would be training me, and I would be prepared to jump through it.

Faithfully God began waking me up in the middle of the night. I could see myself standing at the podium before the group of ladies and I could hear the words that I was speaking. The vision would last awhile and then I would fall back to sleep. Night after night this continued to happen. By the weekend of the retreat, I had written a few notes, but I didn't need to use them, because God had taken me through the words so often that I knew them. He had spent three months training me.

Finally, at the retreat, the moment came for me to walk to the podium, and I visually saw that threatening, burning 'ring of fire' as I faced the group. But then God whispered to my heart, "It's time to run." I fixed my eyes on His and left all thought of fear behind, as I ran and jumped through the fierce flames, and into His waiting arms. The ladies gathered in that room may have seen me physically standing there, and heard me speaking, but in my spirit, I was in my Father's arms and we were dancing all night. He was releasing me from that debilitating fear and was choreographing new breath-taking moves, making me cling to Him even tighter.

There will be days in our lives that will be as wonderful as walking with God in the Garden of Eden. There will also be days that resemble the moment Jesus prayed at the Garden of Gethsemane, with blood-beads of sweat forming on our brow. Offering ourselves and withholding nothing, not even that one most difficult issue, intimately bonds us with the Lover of our soul. God has the ability to bring graceful movement into areas that have been crippling in our lives. We may never resemble Fred Astaire and Ginger Rogers, but as for me, my dance card is full. When my Father takes the lead, no fearsome 'ring of fire' can ever make me stumble in our glorious dance together.

LET'S TALK ~ GOD'S HEART FOR YOU

Have you ever experienced a ring of fire? Something that you know the devil was showing or telling you to bring fear, wrongful thoughts, or burning temptations into your mind? You might remember a song Johnny Cash sang about falling into a ring of fire. Basically, the deeper he fell, the higher the burning flames grew. Surprisingly, the song was not written by Johnny. Instead, it was June Carter, who penned it about their toxic relationship. She wrote that love was a burning thing, because at the time they were married to other people, and Johnny had a serious drug addiction. The whole situation was a flaming fire that was out of control. When Satan fuels the fire, people's lives and marriages are often destroyed. It can send them on a downward spiral to a life of misery and regret.

The 'ring of fire' that Satan conjures up can either send you on that downward spiral to hell-like consequences or send you to seek God's mercy on the situation or temptation. When you are facing the heat of the fire in the midst of the circumstances, it is never an easy decision to make because of the heart-felt passion that is usually involved. You won't see a threatening 'ring of fire' except in the most crucial, gut-wrenching, emotional moments in your life. At that time, your head will be telling you the right thing as your heart is repeating the whisperings of the deceiving devil.

We see that happening in the Garden of Gethsemane with Jesus. Why does the Scripture tell us about the blood drops of sweat on His brow, if there was not an inner turmoil or battle going on inside of Him? Jesus always knew that the Salvation plan to redeem the world would lead to His own suffering and death. But as the time came, Jesus' heart and emotions began to stir in turmoil. The human side of Him was vulnerable to the fear and dread of such a painful death. We can only assume that Satan was whispering and trying to convince Jesus to save Himself.

Jesus was experiencing a 'ring of fire.' We know this to be true because Matthew 26:39 tells us about Jesus in Gethsemane, "Going a little farther, He fell with his face to the ground and prayed,

"My Father, if it is possible, may this cup be taken from me. Yet not as I will, but as you will." We see that He didn't want this coming crucifixion to happen, if at all possible. But Christ aligned His heart and mind to be submissive to His Father's will. He was prepared to jump through the fearsome, flaming 'ring of fire' into His Father's arms.

C. Austin Miles wrote the hymn 'In the Garden.' The story behind the hymn is interesting. In April of 1912, Austin was seated with his Bible opened to his favorite book and chapter, John 20. He shared, "I don't know if this was by chance or by the work of the Holy Spirit. That story of Jesus and Mary in John 20 had lost none of its power and charm. It was as though I was in a trance, as I read it that day; I seemed to be part of the scene." Austin said that he seemed to be standing at the entrance of a garden, looking down a gently winding path, shaded by olive branches. A woman in white, with her head bowed and hand clasping her throat to choke back her sobs, walked slowly. It was Mary. She came to the tomb; she looked in and ran away. Then John and Peter came and went into the tomb. As they left, Mary reappeared and was weeping.

Austin wrote, "Turning, she saw Jesus standing there, so did I. I knew it was He. She knelt before Him, with arms outstretched, and looking into His face cried, *"Rabboni."* I awakened in sunlight, gripping my Bible with my muscles tense, and nerves vibrating, under the inspiration of the Holy Spirit. I wrote as quickly as the words could be formed; that same evening, I wrote the tune."

"I come to the garden alone, while the dew is still on the roses
And the voice I hear, falling on my ear, the Son of God discloses.
And He walks with me and He talks with me, and He tells me I am His own
And the joy we share as we tarry there, none other, has ever known."

His hymn, 'In the Garden,' is sung today exactly as he wrote it in 1912. It was birthed through the Holy Spirit to express that special 'garden fellowship' that God wants with each of us. Generations of believers have loved that song because of the spiritual, emotional sweetness of that beautiful scene of Jesus walking and talking alone with them. There's a preciousness to knowing that you are loved that deeply.

God's heart for you is that you would open your heart and mind to desire more in your relationship with Him. Life-changing God-moments are not to be ignored or forgotten. If you experience a vision, trance, or glimpse of God's supernatural insight, it is meant to bring you closer and join your heart with His own.

1 Corinthians 2:9-12 (NLT) "'No eye has seen, no ear has heard, and no mind has imagined what God has prepared for those who love him.' But it was to us that God revealed these things by his Spirit. For his Spirit searches out everything and shows us God's deep secrets. No one can know a person's thoughts except that person's own spirit, and no one can know God's thoughts except God's own Spirit. And we have received God's Spirit (not the world's spirit), so we can know the wonderful things God has freely given us."

This Scripture encourages us to know there's a lot more to our spiritual life than what we may have yet experienced. God's Holy Spirit dwelling in us searches out everything and reveals (shows us) deep secrets that the world's spirit cannot understand. C. Austin Miles experienced this, and so did I. When the devil wanted to stun me in fear, he showed me a fearsome 'ring of fire.' Then supernaturally, I was shown God's perspective. Through trusting and obeying His will and plan, I found myself in His arms, and we were dancing, not for just an evening, but for a lifetime.

There is no doubt in my mind that if you are reading this, then God has more for you to behold of His glorious nature. He's the lover of your soul, who longs to lead you in the dance of your life. He will whisk you off your feet, bringing you to divine appointments. Scripture says, "no eye has seen, no ear has heard, and no mind has imagined what God has prepared for those who love him." Love the Lord your God with all your heart, all your mind, and all your soul. And He'll walk with you and He'll talk with you; and He'll tell you, you are His own. And the joy you'll share as you tarry there; none other, has ever known.

Reflection: When God romances your heart, will you be willing to jump into His arms, joining Him for the dance of a lifetime?

Meditation music: Dance with Me (as sung by Paul Wilbur) or In the Garden

17

My Ebenezer

ROCK
of
HELP

Have you ever heard God's voice calling your name? Wouldn't that be an amazing experience?

There's a story in the Bible about a young boy who was about twelve years old when it happened to him. God's voice was persistent. 1 Samuel 3:3-10 says, "The lamp of God had not yet gone out, and Samuel was lying down in the temple of the LORD, where the ark of God was. Then the LORD called Samuel. Samuel answered, 'Here I am.' And he ran to Eli (the elderly priest) and said, 'Here I am; you called me.' But Eli said, 'I did not call; go back and lie down.' So, he went and lay down."

Again, the LORD called… [a second time], and then…a third time, "and Samuel got up and went to Eli and said, 'Here I am; you called me.' Then Eli realized that the LORD was calling the boy. So, Eli told Samuel, 'Go and lie down, and if he calls you, say, 'Speak, LORD, for your servant is listening.' So, Samuel went and lay down in his place. The LORD came and stood there, calling as at the other times, 'Samuel! Samuel!' Then Samuel said, 'Speak, for your servant is listening.'" Four times the Lord called his name!

This morning, just before dawn, I awakened to a voice calling me. Over and over in my foggy drowsiness, it persistently tried to rouse me. Slowly I crawled out of bed and walked toward the source. I opened the dog pen and let the barking pup and his two buddies go outside for a few minutes. Soon they were settled back to sleep and I laid back down for some rest, only to hear the words of an old hymn from the 1700s 'Come Thou Fount of Every Blessing' playing through my mind.

"Come thou fount of every blessing; Tune my heart to sing Thy grace
Streams of mercy never ceasing; Call for songs of loudest praise
Teach me some melodious sonnet; Sung by flaming tongues above
Praise the Mount I'm fixed upon it; Mount of Thy redeeming love"

It's an amazing song of God's divine grace. But it was the words from the next verse that seemed to have hit a scratch on the record because I kept hearing the words "Here I raise my Ebenezer, Hither by Thy help I've come."

"Here I raise my Ebenezer; Hither by Thy help I've come
And I hope by Thy good pleasure; Safely to arrive at home"

What in the world is my Ebenezer? I've always wondered about that, and I needed an answer. So, in the dark, at 5:30 am, I found myself reaching for my 'smart phone' on the table beside my bed. Then I googled it. How could I raise my Ebenezer if I didn't even know what it was?

In 1 Samuel 7, the prophet Samuel and the Israelites were about to come under attack by the approaching Philistine army. Fearing for their lives, they asked Samuel to pray to God and beg him for help in this impending battle. God was merciful and gave them great victory, causing the enemy to flee. 1 Samuel 7:12 says "Then Samuel took a stone and set it up...He named it Ebenezer, saying, "Thus far the LORD has helped us." Ebenezer is a Hebrew word which means 'stone of help.'

That mystery was solved, but instead of being able to sleep, I started thinking about a story that was recorded about our local history. It took place nearby and involved the Old Stone House, which is located in Northern Butler County, in Pennsylvania. It was an inn and tavern that had served travelers along a stage-coach line in the 1800s.

At first there didn't seem to be any connection between the song and this historical story except that there was a man named Samuel who was the main character in both. This brief story of the Old Stone House involved an Indian from the Seneca tribe named Samuel Mohawk. Unlike the prophet Samuel in the Bible, who at young age was called by God in the wee hours of the night to serve him, this Samuel lived a troubled life, called by a different master. He had a reputation for drunkenness, violence, and arrests when he traveled in this area over the years as a rafts man.

One morning in July of 1843, an eleven-year-old girl, Catherine Herrit, was walking alone when suddenly she saw an Indian. He pulled out his knife and started chasing her.

Evil had gripped Sam Mohawk's heart and he tried to kill Catherine, but God provided a way for her to escape death. She saw a neighbor's house and quickly ran inside. Angrily, he fled the area. That night, Sam went to the Old Stone House, drank too much, and started a brawling fight with the innkeeper. The innkeeper broke a chair over Sam's head and kicked him out.

Still seething with rage hours later, just after dawn he spotted a light on at the nearby Wigton homestead. He violently attacked and murdered the mother and five children who lived there. Her husband wasn't there to protect them. He had gone to his father's farm to borrow a workhorse. When he returned home hours later, about a hundred enraged neighbors were there. They had already figured out that it must have been Sam Mohawk who committed the horrendous crime, so they formed a posse. The men searched all the surrounding properties and were determined to find Sam and kill him.

Finally, the men found Samuel at a neighbor's house in an upstairs bedroom. Strangely, he was playing a fiddle. The men threw stones at him and knocked him out. Then they dragged Sam out of the house and would have hung him, if the law officer hadn't stopped them. Instead, he was hauled off to the Butler County prison to await trial. Eventually, after a few months, a judge sentenced him to death by hanging.

If you're still reading or listening to my story, I'm sure you are wondering how my thoughts about the song and this historical tale can possibly be connected. It was puzzling me too, although I never doubted God's ability to show me. So I sat on my comfy chair with my morning coffee, pen, and notebook, waiting for His revelation to unfold.

You see, according to Psalm 139:13, Samuel Mohawk was lovingly created by God. He was knitted together in his mother's womb, just like all of us were at one time. He was wonderfully made by our Father. Yet Sam's life story seemed to be in complete rejection of the One who gave him life. His heart was far from God. At some point, Satan, the adversary of his soul, had gained entrance. The door to his heart was left ajar, perhaps by childhood wounds, discrimination, or possibly through some great loss that he suffered. Whatever happened, it allowed uncontained wrath and alcoholism to fill his house, his soul. With Sam being so vulnerable, the devil was able to gain entrance and used him to cause havoc and destruction in the lives of people around him.

In John 10:10, Jesus said, "The thief comes to steal, kill, and destroy..." The enemy tried to use Samuel to kill a young girl, Catherine Herrit, who grew up and married William Protzman. She was my husband's great, great, grandmother. If Catherine would have died, my husband's family would not exist today. But the enemy was unsuccessful, so he made new plans all within a period of twenty-four hours. A day later, early on the following morning, Sam was so extremely driven by that same evil force, that he massacred most of the Wigton family. My great grandfather was Josiah Wigton. I'm a descendant of the family that Sam Mohawk murdered.

Both my husband's and my family lineage were part of the thief's plan to steal, kill, and destroy. But God intervened on our behalf so that our children, grandchildren, and future generations could live to fulfill His plans. None of us would exist otherwise. Yet, "There but for the grace of God, go I," which is a quote from the 1800s that means it is only by God's grace that we haven't walked in Sam's shoes.

> "Jesus, sought me when a stranger; Wandering from the fold of God
> He, to rescue me from danger; Interposed His precious blood"

I was just a child when God interposed His precious blood over me and called my heart to salvation. Jesus sought Sam Mohawk when he was a stranger who had wandered extremely far from the fold of God. While he was in jail waiting for his sentence of death to be carried out, God sent His Holy Spirit to stir up Sam's heart for salvation. He faced an eternity in hell, and many of us would have called that justice for the crime he committed. But God calls sin, sin. We are all guilty. It's only by His grace that we are saved. Sam surrendered to that same grace and became a Christian, according to the historical records. God won the battle against the enemy for Sam's soul, just as He won the battle against the Philistine army to protect His chosen people, the Israelites.

On the day of the execution, an angry mob gathered outside of the prison, and they would have loved to have stoned him to death. But the only one to lift a stone that day was Sam. Samuel Mohawk raised his Ebenezer, the stone of God's help, and he walked by divine grace to the hangman's noose and into eternity with Jesus. Just like the song says, "Safely to arrive at home."

What began early this morning with a voice awakening me just before daylight, led me to weaving together more than just a song and a story of my heritage. It wasn't God's voice calling my name, but He was the One who was calling my heart. He wanted to give me a deeper insight into my life, which Satan attempted to destroy more than 170 years ago.

In John 10:10, the verse about the thief continued with Jesus saying "I came that they may have life and have it abundantly." God preserved my life for me to live it abundantly for Him. He knew that at times I would get distracted, and that I may even be prone to wander away from what he planned for me to do in this life. So He sealed my heart with His Holy Spirit so that my soul would always be drawn back to His love. (Eph.1:13)

"Prone to wander, Lord, I feel it; Prone to leave the
God I love
Here's my heart, Lord, take and seal it; Seal it for Thy
courts above"

I thought that God was wrapping up this story and bringing it to a close. I laid my pen and notebook on my desk and began washing dishes. I began to think about Sam Mohawk in heaven with Jesus and what it must be like for him to finally experience unconditional love and forgiveness. Suddenly the easiness with which I had been writing this story changed. I realized that God had forgiven this man and yet, as far as I knew, my family had never forgiven him. Generations have held onto to the horror of this man's sin and been glad for the justice served.

God prodded my heart to repent of the sin of unforgiveness that has been carried down through all these years. That kind of unforgiveness can plant a deep root of bitterness in people who seem to be vulnerable to Satan's attacks. The bitterness that spews out seems to be unexplainable because there is no apparent reason for it. It stirs up turmoil and causes division in families. It seriously breaks God's heart. So, with tears streaming down my face and with soapy hands, I raised *my Ebenezer,* the stone of God's help, and I forgave Sam on behalf of all my ancestors who hated him. I asked God to forgive our family for our unforgiveness and to break the generational curse caused by our sin. Thank you, God, for Your great mercy over us. Lamentations 3:22-23 tells us "Because of the LORD's great love we are not consumed, for His compassions never fail. They are new every morning; great is Your faithfulness."

"Here I raise my Ebenezer; Hither by Thy help I come
And I hope by Thy good pleasure; Safely to
arrive at home"

LET'S TALK ~ GOD'S HEART FOR YOU

God created you to bring Him glory. Psalms 139:13-14 says, "For you created my inmost being; you knit me together in my mother's womb. I praise you because I am fearfully and wonderfully made." God made you unique and like no one else. He proudly knitted you together to be His child, so you could enter this world and make a difference in the lives of your family and friends.

Jeremiah 29:11 declares, "For I know the plans I have for you," declares the LORD, "plans to prosper you and not to harm you, plans to give you hope and a future." God instilled in you talents and a personality that would allow you to be able to fulfill His purpose and the plans that He established for your life. You are loved and very important to God.

Ephesians 2:10 tells us, "For we are God's handiwork, created in Christ Jesus to do good works, which God prepared in advance for us to do." This Scripture affirms that God created us to be one with Christ. We were always meant to be walking in the power that we have received through our redemption. It's in Christ, in knowing Him intimately, that we are given the authority to do the good works that God prepared for us. Those plans are beyond our ability to carry out in our own strength and wisdom.

God created us so perfectly, yet from an early age we fall away from that perfection, because of the original sin of Adam and Eve. Toddlers don't need to be taught to disobey, and they don't need to learn how to tell little lies to keep themselves from getting into trouble with their parents. That sinful nature is something that we are born into; it's in our DNA. The curse of sin has been on mankind and all living things since that fateful moment in the garden when temptation became irresistible to Adam and Eve. God has given us free choice. We can choose to follow Jesus Christ, or we can reject Him. In every person, God has deposited a restless longing for the empty place in our soul to be filled with His Spirit. If you reject Jesus and choose to go your own way, you will be walking through life in opposition to God's plan. More than likely, it will not go well in the long run. You will be void of the power of the Holy Spirit, which God has designated for you to embrace. It is through His Holy Spirit that you can accomplish everything that He has planned for you. With His Spirit ruling your life, amazing, unexplainable things will happen.

Still, you need to beware of the enemy who will attempt to derail you. If you are trying to live life on your own terms, you will be an easy target to manipulate. If that is the case, you are probably already doing his bidding, unknowingly. If you are a believer, the devil will work even harder to distract you from the righteous path set before you. He is crafty and will do everything he can to divert your attention from following God's perfect plan.

John 10:10 (ESV) "The thief comes only to steal and kill and destroy. I came that they may have life, and have it abundantly." (The thief is our adversary) The adversary of our soul is Lucifer, who is also known as Satan or the Devil. He was an angel who became very prideful and schemed to become God so that he could take over His Heavenly Throne. He wanted to rule the universe and everything in it. He had cleverly lured other angels to trust and follow him. But when he finally rebelled, God overpowered him. Satan was thrown out of heaven along with about a third of the angels (millions) who followed him. He was humiliated and defeated. He will do everything in his power to keep you from receiving Jesus Christ as your Savior. He hates that you love God. The enemy has lots of help–an army of fallen angels to help him tempt you and derail you. Never underestimate his cleverness and deceitfulness. He thoroughly hates God and will try everything to destroy or kill you.

Unforgiveness (our stubborn refusal to forgive) is a tool of manipulation that Satan powers-up against us. He uses it to try to block our relationship with God. There are consequences to the act of unforgiveness, which we read in Matthew 6:14-15. "For if you forgive other people when they sin against you, your heavenly Father will also forgive you. But if you do not forgive others their sins, your Father will not forgive your sins." The Bible is very clear that if we stubbornly hold unforgiveness against anyone, God will not forgive us. Intentionally refusing to forgive someone builds an invisible barrier that keeps us from having a deep, intimate relationship with God. It breaks His heart.

God's heart for you is that you would forgive people of any offenses that they have done to you over the years. Forgiveness breaks the stronghold of the enemy in our life and in the life of the one we have forgiven. That release brings a freedom that God will use to work out His perfect will. Forgiveness and restoration bring back God's blessing for the abundant life we were created to live. "And God is able to bless you abundantly, so that in all things at all times, having all that you need, you will abound in every good work." 2 Corinthians 9:8 Having received the abundance of God, you will succeed in every good work God sets before you to do. The fruit of your life accomplishments will bring Him honor and glory, which fulfills the reason why God created you.

Reflection: God can restore impossible relationships if we are willing to open our hearts to forgive people. Will you trust God's faithfulness to help you now?

Meditation music: Forgiveness or Come, Thou Fount of Every Blessing

18

Little Princess

A few days ago, I came across an old DVD on my shelf by Nicole Johnson, who has written and performed skits for Christian women's conferences. As I watched it, I laughed and I cried, especially during "Princess in Pajamas." It started with an old film clip of a little girl whose smile revealed missing front teeth. She received a tiara from her daddy when he returned from a business trip. He crowned her 'Princess Callie.' Her elation of being his little princess filled the home video with the pure, innocent delight of a child's dream come true. She was her daddy's princess no matter what she was doing-riding her bike, or still playing in her pajamas. She wore her crown as if it was always meant for her to wear.

Yet the fairy tale came to an abrupt end, far too quickly, when her dad announced that he would not be returning from his next business trip. When he left, he stole her childhood innocence. He packed his luggage with her trust, hope, and dreams. He stuffed inside the bag her image of self-worth; then he sat on the case as he zipped in all the security that was meant to protect the delicate life of his child.

After I watched the skit, I thought about my own life. My parents had three boys and then, finally, I was born. Being the first girl, my daddy always made me feel extra special, like I was royalty. I knew that he delighted in me. I remember when I was little, sometimes he would take my hand and we would walk to the outdoor shed. There he would hitch our garden tractor to a large wooden wagon so he could give my siblings and all the neighborhood kids a ride.

There was a wide wooden board across the front of the wagon where my dad would sit to drive. He always picked me up and sat me next to him, when the wagon was filling up with kids. It was a place of honor, reserved just for me.

For many years, my dad drove me to my piano lessons. Being country folks, our social life centered around friends and family gathering for picnics or having a game night. We had visitors often. My dad would always tell them, "Come listen to the song my daughter can play on the piano." They would gather around the piano in the living room and I'd take my place on the piano bench and sit up tall and proper. I'd curve my fingers, and I'd be as impressive as possible while I played my little tune. Then I would wait for the expected applause. Always, even if I missed a few notes, my dad's smile gleamed and I could see that he felt proud of me. I didn't need a visible tiara to know I was his princess.

But through the years, unknown to my father, life began to tarnish my crown through times of bullying and secret abuse that were stealing away my childhood innocence. When I was seventeen, my dad passed away from cancer. I can still remember the heartbreak of losing him and my great sorrow. Looking back, I can see it was a time when my tiara became unattached; all that had held it securely in place had slipped away from this world. Life had packed it away, sat on the lid to force it in, then zipped it into obscurity.

After watching the DVD with my friends, I realized my story was sad, but I was more heartbroken when a friend said "I went from the womb into a barrel of whiskey." Basically, she meant that alcohol was the cruel king that ruled in her home throughout her childhood. Another friend remained completely silent. Later, she privately shared with me, "I was never special to anybody." Neither had experienced love like I had.

There's an old saying that "It's better to have loved and lost than to have never loved at all." It's not from the Bible but there is a lot of truth in that statement. I experienced a father's love that made me know that I was special. Even after he died and I lost the love of my father, I could still remember how that unconditional love felt.

Some have never experienced that extraordinary love of a parent that esteems and encourages them. As little children, there is something in us that makes us long for that acclamation which causes us to feel special. Little girls aspiring to be princesses and little boys striving to be king of the hill in their games are subtly driven by something inside that needs to be nurtured and fulfilled.

Could it be the same component of emptiness that keeps us searching for our completeness, which can only be found in Jesus Christ? Could our self-worth ever be perfected until we see ourselves through the eyes of God? How much harder it must be for people to receive our heavenly Father's love and believe that God takes great delight in them if they have never received it from an earthly father. Scripture assures us that "The LORD your God is with you, He will take great delight in you;" Zephaniah 3:17.

There's a story in the Bible (Luke 15:8-10) about a lost coin that is diligently searched for because it is precious and valuable. No matter how much work and time it takes, that coin is never forgotten. The owner never gives up their rightful claim to possess what was meant to be theirs. We belong to God, our heavenly Father. We have been rightfully His from the beginning of time. He never gives up on us.

Sometimes, however, we fall through the cracks of life-between the floorboards-and darkness shadows over us. The light of truth is hidden from us. Sometimes we are victims of circumstances and a life that has treated us harshly. Sometimes that separation from the light becomes normal life to us.

Yet it's not the life that was intended for us to live. So, God placed a longing in each soul that could only be satisfied by His Presence. Even if we don't understand what is driving it, it's there. God's Word says He created us to be His children, but we are given the right to choose. He prepared a kingdom for us–an everlasting kingdom. He calls us to actively participate in it and to reign with Him. It's only through the power of the Holy Spirit, covered by the righteousness of Christ, that we can take our rightful place as a prince or a princess in our Father's royal domain.

Our experiences in this life contribute to the uniqueness of who God created us to be throughout our present and eternal life. Every bad and difficult experience, God can redeem to fortify the strength of our testimony. He transforms their negative effect into a display of His love and splendor. Becoming a daughter, of the Most High King, crowned me with a tiara that can never be tarnished or packed into a suitcase and stolen from me again. I'm pretty sure that most folks around me are blind to the bling of the embedded diamonds intertwined by lacy white gold that adorns my head. Nevertheless, I know it's there because every now and then, I see a flash of God's reflective light radiating from it.

At times, my heavenly Father takes my hand and lifts me up to sit beside him in a place of honor. He reminds me that, like my earthly father, He has driven me to lessons all my life so that I may be taught by the Word. He surrounds me with a 'great cloud of witnesses' (Hebrews 12:1) and says, "Come listen to my daughter as she plays the song of my grace and redemption that I wrote for her to play." They gather around me as I sit on the bench to display His splendor. I assume the position expected of me. As I sit tall and proper, fingers curved, God places a royal scepter of authority in my hand so that I may reign with power in this life. Concentrating on the composition set before me to play, I'm encouraged by glimpses of my Father smiling. He's delighted. I'm His little princess. Someday as my song ends, I will anticipate the applause of the saints in heaven. And at that time, I will join them to applaud my Father, the King of all Kings.

LET'S TALK ~ GOD'S HEART FOR YOU

God sees all the times when you have suffered. He knows when you've been mistreated, and He knows what has wounded your soul. The Lord understands all the circumstances that may have caused brokenness in your heart. Lovingly, He wants to comfort you. Our Father promises to give you peace in every past situation that continues to crush your spirit. Psalm 34:18 tells us that "The Lord is near to the brokenhearted and saves the crushed in spirit." "He heals the brokenhearted and binds up their wounds." Psalm 147:3

Jesus promises that He will carry your heavy cares, worries, and whatever weighs your heart down. Surrendering all the hurt and pain can be difficult. You may need to picture yourself laying all those troubling things at His feet. He promises us rest from it. Jesus tells us to "Come to me, all of you who are weary and carry heavy burdens, and I will give you rest." Matthew 11:28 (NLT)

God rightfully owns us; He created us. He shines a light for us when we have fallen through the cracks of difficulties or sin and are hidden by a dark shadow. Our Father never gives up on us when we are lost. Scripture tells us that He sends His Holy Spirit to woe us and to stir up our hearts for salvation. Then He gathers the angels to rejoice with Him over that moment when we become His child, and God crowns us with His grace.

Luke 15:8-10 "Suppose a woman has ten silver coins and loses one. Doesn't she light a lamp, sweep the house and search carefully until she finds it? And when she finds it, she calls her friends and neighbors together and says, 'Rejoice with me; I have found my lost coin.' In the same way, I tell you, there is rejoicing in the presence of the angels of God over one sinner who repents."

As God brings healing and forgiveness of the past, it's important that we train ourselves to keep our eyes focused on what God is preparing for our future. He transforms us to see ourselves as He sees us. In Philippians 3:13-14 (ESV), Paul tells us one thing he had to do: "Forgetting what lies behind and straining forward to what lies ahead, I press on toward the goal for the prize of the upward call of God in Christ Jesus."

Perhaps you had a rough childhood and never experienced the extravagant love of a parent who encouraged and took special interest in you. It's never too late for God to redeem the past and give you a glimpse of the smile and joy you bring to His heart. His unconditional love accepts you at this very moment and sees you as precious. Our Father takes great delight in you. He loves you, sings over you, and rejoices that you belong to him. He has saved and redeemed you. Zephaniah 3:17 "The Lord your God is with you, the Mighty Warrior who saves. He will take great delight in you; in His love he will no longer rebuke you, but will rejoice over you with singing."

When we fear God and have a healthy relationship with Him, we can know that our sins are cleansed by Jesus' blood. God no longer rebukes us because of our sinfulness or mistakes. He has thrown those things as far as the east is from the west and remembers them no more. His great love is far beyond our ability to fully comprehend.

Psalm 103:11-12 "For as high as the heavens are above the earth, so great is his love for those who fear him; as far as the east is from the west, so far has he removed our transgressions from us."

Often, we have trouble letting go of our own guilt. God blots out our sin for His sake because He desires a relationship with us. That is why our Father sees us through the righteous blood of His son, Jesus. He chooses not to remember our sin because it would keep us separated from Him. Isaiah 43:25 (NKJV) tells us, "I, even I, am He who blots out your transgressions for My own sake; And I will not remember your sins."

We are God's people, His sons and daughters, His princes and princesses. Our heavenly Father is King; and we are royalty in His kingdom. God loves us!

"For the Lord takes delight in his people; he crowns the humble with victory." Psalm 149:4 On your head, He places a crown that illuminates His marvelous work of redemption and the anointing power poured over you. You were always meant to be His little princess (prince). The crown signifies that you belong to the King. And it declares that everlasting victory has been won for you through Jesus Christ.

Reflection: Do you see yourself as God sees you? You are His price-less treasure, His royal child, whom He has lovingly redeemed! You need to see yourself as blessed, and highly favored by your Father, the King!

Meditation music: We Fall Down or A Child of the King

19.

THE GOLD COIN

It's probably a weird personality quirk along with some attention deficit issues, but when I visit a different church or go to a seminar, it takes me a while to become focused. Over the weekend I attended a retreat, and after I left the first session, I realized that I had spent the evening analyzing the effectiveness of the speaker.

I had watched those around me and weighed their responses and reactions to her. She had told hilarious stories to enhance the message, but was it balanced? Was there enough Scriptural teaching, and did it encourage this group by touching a need in their life? Afterwards, while we were walking down the hall in the hotel complex, I was still contemplating whether the evening had met my expectations to be a successful retreat for all the ladies. For some reason, I was reacting like it was my job to be the appointed spiritual overseer instead of being there to participate myself.

The next morning, after a restless night of sleep, I was too tired to try to analyze it all again, so I just relaxed and listened. It was actually very inspiring. Finally, after I was able to abandon all of the earlier distractions from the night before, I was able to feel the presence of God. Later, the afternoon session began with a worship segment. It felt strange to be among the singing crowd, and it took me a while to loosen up enough to use my hands to clap with everyone else. Normally my comfort zone was using my hands to play the keyboard with the praise team, but now I wanted to fit in with the other ladies.

As I raised my voice and heart in adoration to the Lord, unexpectedly I felt my hand being drawn up toward heaven. With one arm already up, before long it was all I could do to keep the other arm down, secured to my side and under control. It seemed to be magnetized by something above and it was also being pulled high, parallel to the other. As soon as it happened, my mind flashed to another time zone of the old west and my childhood memories of tv westerns, and I automatically said, "Okay Lord, I give up; I surrender!" And He said, "That's what I've been waiting for."

I stood there in that awkward stance until the music ended, repeating over and over those same words as my hands remained above my head. I felt like a bandit who had robbed the bank and had been tracked down by the Marshall. I knew exactly what the crime was that I had committed, and I knew that He held the evidence against me.

You see, there have been things in my life that God has asked me to give up and give to him for a season. Each of those things was like a pure, solid gold coin, a treasure that I had offered him. He stored them in a special vault for safekeeping, but during the dark of night I slipped into the bank and snatched one back, hoping He wouldn't notice. Surely one little gold piece wouldn't matter that much to the big-time Banker. My intentions were to return it eventually; I just wanted to enjoy it for a while. Most people carry that very same coin guilt-free because it's not something bad, but it was one of the things that the Lord had asked me to surrender to Him for a while. He had his reasons and this was a matter of my willingness to be obedient.

A couple of mornings before the retreat, I was working on a ministry project and I began hearing the words, "You can't walk un-surrendered." It sounded like a double negative. Would the Lord really speak like that? As I continued to think about it, I realized that God had spoken it exactly how he meant it, and the point became clear. Weeks before the retreat, I had taken back something precious. He hadn't given it back to me. It was an act of un-surrender that would stifle my spiritual effectiveness and keep me at a standstill. My feet might continue to shuffle some but there would be little progress.

Psalm 32:1-2,5,10 says, "Blessed is the one whose transgressions are forgiven, whose sins are covered. Blessed is the one whose sin the Lord does not count against them and in whose spirit is no deceit. Then I acknowledged my sin to you and did not cover up my iniquity. I said, "I will confess my transgressions to the Lord." And you forgave the guilt of my sin. Many are the woes of the wicked, but the Lord's unfailing love surrounds the one who trusts in him."

This passage makes it clear that I am not fully blessed, the way God wants to bless me, when I am walking un-surrendered. For me, while I was busy analyzing everyone else at the ladies' retreat, I was also being analyzed by God. Catching me off guard, the Lord knew it was the right moment to corner me. He had been wearing me down for weeks, and in my heart, I knew that it was only a matter of time until the confrontation. While the other women raised their hands in praise and worship, mine were raised in guilty surrender. All around me they were singing beautiful words, looking joyful and glowing in the presence of God.

Meanwhile, I looked like a bristly, out of place thorn among the lovely roses. I could only squirm and mutter "I give up; I surrender" over and over as tears streaked brown mascara down my face. At the time it was an awkward, ugly scene for me. But looking back now, I know that nothing else that I could have offered my Father would have touched His heart as that moment of repentance. It was my ultimate act of worship; It was what He was requiring from me. It carried back to my Father the precious gold coin, the piece of my heart that He was missing.

LET'S TALK ~ GOD'S HEART FOR YOU

According to Psalm 32, we are blessed when our spirit is cleansed from any deceit and we've been forgiven. God knows that we are all guilty of sin, so His hand continues to apply pressure to weaken our stubbornness that causes us to hold onto it. In confessing our crimes, we are no longer held prisoner and locked-in behind barred doors caused by our wrongful actions. We are released into God's protective custody, and soothed by His joyful songs of deliverance.

God's heart for you is that there would be no issues that are unresolved in your relationship with Him. Sometimes the problem is not a blatant sin but a mindset of independence that keeps you walking on your own path in life that is not God's direction for you. It's an okay trail, but it's not the best route that He planned. Whatever it is that keeps you from His complete will for your life is not worth the loss of missing all the amazing adventures ahead. Don't remain un-surrendered; raise your arms and let it go. It will be like a piece of your heart being returned back to God, like a precious, pure gold coin that belongs in His heavenly vault. You will never regret it.

The Lord promises to guide and give you direction so that you can once again move ahead into the future He ordained for you. Surrounded by your Father's great love, you will have a restored, upright heart that freely worships Him. "Rejoice in the Lord and be glad, you righteous; sing, all you who are upright in heart!" Psalm 32:11

Reflection: Am I willing to release my stubborn control in order to live my life surrendered to God's will? Lord, please forgive me and touch me with your grace.

Meditation music: Holy Water or There is Power in the Blood

20.

His Beloved

To everything there is a season, and a time for every purpose under heaven:

A time to be born...and a time to die;

A time to plant, and a time to harvest;

A time to kill, and a time to heal;

A time to tear down, and a time to build up;

A time to cry, and a time to laugh;

A time to mourn, and a time to dance. Ecclesiastes 3:1-4 (NLT)

Ah, the wisdom of King Solomon, who wrote these words as he reminisced over his life. Each phase of time is completed by its direct contrast but what lies in between often remains to be an untold story. Each person experiences every season in these time segments. All are ordered precisely for an exact moment destined to fit on the dotted road from birth to death. It's that journey that holds the secret to its 'purpose under heaven', exposing the significance of our life accomplishments.

Just like Solomon, there is much to ponder as we reminisce over the various seasons in our lives. My thoughts are drawn toward my favorite season in nature, which is fall. Summertime, full of its lush shades of green, has begun to be transformed. Grass and flowers touched by frost quickly die off, but the leaves of trees take a different journey that is breathtaking. God plans a spectacular hurrah for them as he seemingly commissions Michelangelo to once again pick up his paint brush and lavish the earth with vibrant color, His hand creating a masterpiece. But instead of taking years to complete like the Sistine Chapel in Italy, it only takes weeks. As we behold the finished work, God's splendor is displayed in His unlimited magnificence. Only God could have planned it so perfectly, for "Great is our Lord and mighty in power; His understanding (ability) has no limit." Ps.147:5

Last fall, we had planned to travel during the week when the leaves were at their peak of change, but our lives took an unexpected detour. My only view of that beautiful landscape was through the back window of an ambulance as I traveled from a hospital to a rehabilitation center one afternoon. But as sad as those circumstances were, I found myself praising God. I was filled with a sweet delight during that hour of escape from confined rooms, for I had been through major surgery, life and death complications, several ambulance trips and weeks in three different hospitals.

That beautiful season had morphed into a desolate one. I found myself in a time of mourning. For without warning, I was in the midst of a complete loss of control over my life. But through those grim circumstances, God was faithful. He gave me visions of hope and of His love, not only through an ambulance window framing fall colors, but through ministering angels and compassionate people.

Often, I thought about my tomorrows—would I have any? "How do you know what your life will be like tomorrow? Your life is like the morning fog—it's here a little while, then it's gone...If the Lord wants us to, we will live..." says James 4:14-15 (NLT). In those quiet moments of unspoken thoughts, God comforted me. He reminded me that every day of my life was written in His book when He created me. If He wills, I will live to be ancient, if not, I will be with Him.

My life was suddenly extremely fragile. There were hundreds of people praying for me. God gave me His peace that passes all understanding. I felt strangely secure for I knew that I was "dwelling in the secret place of the Most High, abiding under the shadow of the Almighty." Psalm 91:1 (KJV) Even when I was laying on a stretcher for hours in an emergency room, not knowing if I would live or die, I felt peaceful.

Meanwhile, my family was frantically trying to get a doctor to come help me. And they were helping the nurse get my medical records in order, so that I could be transferred to a different hospital. The first nurse helping me couldn't handle the pressure of what was happening. She was replaced by a more experienced male nurse. He came in the room and began working on me and said, "How can you be so calm?" Without hesitation, words flew out of my mouth, "Jesus is here with me." He gave me a startled look, staring at me for a moment. Then, the truth of those words brought me into an even deeper peace. I knew that the presence of God would never leave me nor forsake me, just as He promised in His Word.

Although I wasn't happy to be in that weakened condition of helplessness, I never doubted that somehow, it was all part of God's plan. Through my ongoing trauma, I was taken by ambulance to a large Pittsburgh hospital in the middle of the night. But later that day, I was rejected from that second hospital because of medical insurance issues. They found a surgeon at a different hospital who agreed to accept my case. So, I was moved again by ambulance later that evening.

The situation made us feel really angry. Yet as we look back, we know that God was working out His better plan for me. At that third hospital, God sent me his beloved Mancini. No, it wasn't another famous Italian artist or an exquisite pasta dish, but His beloved daughter. God created Dr. Sheri Anne Mancini with great intelligence, skillful hands, and an amazing heart of compassion. Before she was born, He knew the details of every day of her life yet to come, the ones lived and the ones yet to be. He filled her with courage and the daring to engage where others of lesser determination would shrink back and retreat. "For we are God's masterpiece. He has created us anew in Christ Jesus, so we can do the good things He planned for us long ago." Eph. 2:10 (NLT)

In my imaginings, I have pictured her as a little girl playing doctor, bandaging her teddy bear and doll from her tiny black plastic doctor bag. Dressed up in an oversized white coat pulled from her parent's closet, even then she was filled with a deep yearning to fix lives. In reality, I don't know anything about her childhood dreams, nor her life growing up, nor her career, except for what I have read about her background. Dr. Mancini served as a surgeon in the U.S. Navy, providing routine, emergency, and trauma care for more than 5,000 military personnel as the only surgeon for an air craft carrier and its associated destroyers. She was also deployed to Iraq as a field trauma surgeon for the U.S. Marines. God protected her through many horrific, dangerous situations. He designed her with a great feistiness and a fearlessness to get her hands into bloody messes to save people's lives. I know that she walks in a dynamic anointing of God-given favor. Her life reminds me of Psalms 144:1 "Praise be to the LORD my Rock, who trains my hands for war, my fingers for battle." For the Lord has trained her for battle and has established the work of her hands.

And she has been mercifully faithful to that calling that indwells her spirit.

Last fall, after three weeks of rehabilitation and still feeling deathly sick, I was rushed to the emergency room again. Dr. Mancini spent over five hours working on me through a difficult emergency surgery. God saved my life by her gifted hands, and I will be forever grateful.

Even though I've had great struggles, I know "that in all things, God works for the good of those who love Him, who have been called according to His purpose" Romans 8:28, for I have loved Jesus since I was a little girl. And as I reminisce over my life, like King Solomon, my faith is renewed. As his father David wrote, "Each day the Lord pours His unfailing love upon me, and through each night I sing His songs, praying to God who gives me life." Psalm 42:8 (NLT)

Over these past six months, God has been healing and strengthening me as I am preparing to have one more major surgery. Through prayer, I have approached His throne of grace with confidence, so that I could receive mercy to help me in my time of need. In that need, God sent me His beloved doctor because I am His beloved daughter. Already, a great measure of His mercy has been poured over me as He has transitioned my life from a time of mourning to a time of dancing. As I have been recuperating, He has been transforming my mind and filling me with vision for Hope House Ministries. He has set my feet a-dancing to develop the new ideas that he has given me in this spring-summer season.

The Lord gave me a new direction for our ladies' summer program and it has been amazing. God has been bringing new life to a book that I have been writing, but never completed, called, "As Taught by My Father." Perhaps I have more lessons to learn. God has been helping me to assemble another project that will not only affect the lives of people in this time and season but will help them create a legacy of faith for future generations. I know that God is the mastermind behind my thoughts. Through the cycle of my life, His plan exceeds any that I could ever imagine, for whatever time or season that I am in, I am content.

Knowing that I can trust my Father's great love for me, there's no need for me to worry about tomorrow, for my lifespan, that flows between birth and death, has already been masterfully painted onto the canvas of my destiny. The significance of my life and my untold story will be revealed precisely as God decides. For it is written, "To everything there is a season, a time for every purpose under heaven." As God wills it, so be it...Amen.

LET'S TALK ~ GOD'S HEART FOR YOU

The opening of my story, Ecclesiastes 3:1-4, points out that we all will go through many seasons in this lifetime. It's not optional; it's truth—since God included it in His Book. We need His wisdom and guidance to be prepared for each changing season.

There's an old hymn, 'God Leads Us Along,' that I could relate to during that dark, winter season in my life. It tells how the Lord leads His dear children through shady, green pastures or sometimes on the mount where the sun shines so bright. But when you come to the chorus, it reveals a glimpse of another path where God leads us that isn't so pleasant or endearing. "Some through the waters, some through the flood, some through the fire, but all through the blood; Some through great sorrow, but God gives a song, in the night season and all the day long."

I'm fairly sure that God doesn't really enjoy taking us down paths that lead to difficult times in our lives, but we all have, or will go through, unexpected and unwelcomed situations. They may be filled with turmoil, pain, tears, and a lot of desperate pleading for God's mercy. That's what I experienced, and His mercy saved me from an early death. When He brought Dr. Mancini into my situation, I was the victim of a botched surgery which left me spiraling to near death. I remember thinking that if I had to live the rest of my life feeling this awful, I'd prefer to die and be with Jesus. After my emergency surgery, while in the ICU, they said that I was so dehydrated that they thought my kidneys had shut down. They also told me that I was only one point away from having malnutrition. As a result of the trauma, meds, and countless x-rays, two-thirds of my hair fell out while I was recovering at home for months, under the care of visiting nurses. It was a night season in my life, but as the hymn promises–through great sorrow, God gives a song. I may never fully recover my strength, but in my weakness, He has been strong. In mercy, God faithfully continues to sing a song of grace over me when I have days of discouragement. He gently soothes my heart with His melody of love. I am blessed by my Father's care.

What does God's mercy look like in your life during trials? I've had a longtime friend, Becky, who has always had the boldness and audacity to come face to face with people who were going through difficult personal times and say, "So, what is God showing you through this?" Let me tell you, she has made several people instantly livid, including my husband and our former pastor. After both survived the blunt force of the unexpected question, they did look at their trial in light of God's mercy and learned what He wanted them to understand. They realized Becky was God's messenger, not the devil's advocate. She was often a blessing in disguise and we loved her for her gumption and fearlessness to help us to mature in God's wisdom and grace.

No doubt, in your life you have experienced trials. Sometimes it's an extremely long season that could be described as a 'dark night of the soul.' King David went through seasons like that, according to the Bible. Often his testimony seemed like a tug of war between hopelessness and hope, great sorrow and rejoicing. Reading through many of His writings in the book of Psalm, it is obvious that betrayal, rejection, living in fear of death threats, and seeking safety in the wilderness places took a toll on his soul. Yet, by the end of each chapter, his soul was restored by God's merciful love to know that this time would pass into a new season. And he would indeed see the goodness of the Lord in the land of the living.

In Psalm 27:13-14 David wrote: "I remain confident of this: I will see the goodness of the Lord in the land of the living. Wait for the Lord; be strong and take heart and wait for the Lord." David knew that even though his enemies seemed to be winning the battle to suppress and destroy him, God would prevail. But he would have to endure by faith and trust God knowing that his life was subject to God's timing. He patiently waited for the Lord.

Philippians 4:6-7 "Do not be anxious about anything, but in every situation, by prayer and petition, with thanksgiving, present your requests to God. And the peace of God, which transcends all understanding, will guard your hearts and your minds in Christ Jesus."

Pray, worship and praise God for everything. Pour out your heart to Him. When you feel the most helpless and you know that you have no control over whatever is happening in your life, surrender it to God's authority. Surrendering is a deliberate decision to give all your anxieties and worries to God. It's an act of releasing your death-grip on those plaguing issues that the enemy has convinced you to believe are a part of your life. He's fooled you to believe it's your responsibility to learn to deal with them. But that's a lie that keeps you restrained from having your arms fully open to receive and hold God's supernatural peace. His peace is like "dwelling in the secret place of the Most High, abiding under the shadow of the Almighty." Ps.91:1 (NKJ) The peace of God is surreal and truly indescribable.

Eph. 2:10 (NLT) "For we are God's masterpiece. He has created us anew in Christ Jesus, so we can do the good things He planned for us long ago." You are God's masterpiece. He created you with talent, skills, and a unique personality. And He made good plans for your life before you were born. For example, my doctor may be a Christian, or she may not be. Either way, God gave her the intelligence, the determination, and natural ability to become an excellent skilled surgeon. Through her dedication to save lives, God has blessed her and blessed many people.

If you are a Christian, not only do you have those special assets God created in you as he formed you, but there's more. When you are filled with the Holy Spirit, you experience supernatural giftings that seem to be out of the wheel-house of your competency or expertise. When you trust God and live beyond yourself, then you become a display of God's splendor and His glory. What God accomplishes through you becomes an inspiration for others. It draws people's hearts to desire all that God created them to become by His power.

As God orchestrates this life on earth, you will never have all the answers and probably won't understand His thoughts and ways. Sometimes you may even question the purpose of the hardships and disappointments that you have endured. But always remember that God has blessings in store for you. And as you walk out your life according to His will, you can be certain that God has set the seasons of your life to occur at His precise timing. You can know "that in all things, God works for the good of those who love Him, who have been called according to His purpose." God has your good in mind. YOU are His Beloved.

Reflection: Have I surrendered my will, concerning the hardships and disappointments in my life, to God's higher thoughts and plans to work in those situations?

Meditation music: Blessings (Laura Story) or God Leads Us Along

21.

Towels in my Closet

One evening, I was helping my daughter-in-law fold a huge basket of towels. I came across one of the towels that I had given my son when he moved into a rented house before his wedding. Knowing that he would be getting some for wedding gifts, I gave him just a few out of my closet to tide him over. Each time I folded one of them, I had endearing thoughts of my son, still using the ones his 'Mom' had given him. Sentimentally, I commented about them still using my towels although they had beautiful new ones. Then my daughter-in-law said, "Oh, now we just use those to clean up messes and wipe the floor from wet boots." Immediately, I felt a little irritated, thinking, "How could they use them as rags? They're as good as the ones we use every day...maybe I'll set that small stack aside, and return them back to my own closet."

Fortunately, I was biting my tongue and kept silent. No one knew I was riled up but God. I stewed over it until the next morning when I opened my bathroom closet and looked at my stack of towels. Before me was a rainbow of colors; some were vivid and bold, others were pastel, striped, or flowered. As I stood there, God began to speak to my heart that those towels were like the spiritual gifts He has given us through the Holy Spirit. There's such a variety.

In I Corinthians 12:4-11 (NASB), Paul wrote about the gifts of the Holy Spirit. "Now there are varieties of gifts, but the same Spirit. And there are varieties of ministries, and the same Lord. There are varieties of effects, but the same God who works all things in all persons. But to each one is given the manifestation of the Spirit for the common good. For to one, is given *the word of wisdom* through the Spirit, and to another *the word of knowledge* according to the same Spirit; to another *faith* by the same Spirit, and to another *gifts of healing* by the one Spirit, and to another *the effecting of miracles*, and to another *prophecy*, and to another *the distinguishing of spirits*, to another *various kinds of tongues*, and to another *the interpretation of tongues*. But one and the same Spirit works all these things, distributing to each one individually just as He wills."

These are all supernatural gifts which are supernaturally empowered. Nobody can teach themselves or be trained to have these gifts. It's good for us to desire them, but it's the choice of the Holy Spirit to decide which gift or gifts He will give us. They are given to strengthen and minister to the body of Christ, which helps us to mature in our faith. These gifts are the manifestation of the Holy Spirit, who dwells in us.

Paul writes about the church body being united as the body of Christ.

1 Corinthians 12:12,14 (NLT) "The human body has many parts, but the many parts make up one whole body. So, it is with the body of Christ... But we have all been baptized into one body by one Spirit, and we all share the same Spirit."

Paul continued to break down each body part, and its necessary function for the wellness of the whole body. He used an analogy of the human body, and the importance of each part, to correlate to the body of believers and the unique gift He places in each person. There must be a respect and a rightful place for each gift to be utilized. Otherwise, the body will be lacking and less effective in the ministry that God has ordained for it.

As I looked over other Scriptures that list some other gifts, my thoughts returned to that stack of towels in my closet. I thought about the extra special ones that I have placed out of reach for everyday use. They are reserved for special occasions and for company. Because of my habit of not using them, sometimes I completely forget to pull them out until it's too late. God began to turn my attention to examine my own life. Have I done that with my spiritual gift, and has the church body done the same thing? Are there gifts that we have placed out of reach and have forgotten about, like my extra special towels for company? Have we downgraded others that seemed less valuable, like my ex-towels, until there is a mess on the floor to clean up? Are we really utilizing all that God has made available to us, or is God feeling disappointed or irritated that we no longer use some of them? Has He thought about setting them aside, and returning them to His own closet?

LET'S TALK ~ GOD'S HEART FOR YOU

This morning I was listening to the Scriptures while I was knitting a scarf for a fundraiser. I had played the same passage over several times, when I realized that it was the perfect wrap-up for this story. God is so faithful in leading my thoughts and showing me perfect verses to use. Often, He confirms it several times. This was the same verse that I had read yesterday in a daily devotional book. 2 Timothy 1:6 (NLT) "This is why I remind you to fan into flames the spiritual gift God gave you when I laid my hands on you."

While in prison, the Apostle Paul wrote a letter of encouragement to Timothy, whom he loved as a son. Paul had been mentoring him to be a leader in the church. He started the letter by reminding Timothy about the legacy of faith of his grandmother and mother. Paul told him that same faith was within him. It was important for Timothy to walk in a level of faith that was strong enough to actively fan the flames of his spiritual gift. His gift would be supernaturally powered by the Holy Spirit. It would propel Timothy forward in ministry to be able to accomplish everything that God had planned for him to do.

My son Mark, who I gave those towels to years ago, has been learning the trade of forging steel. He was fascinated by a reality show on the History channel called Forged in Fire. That show has taken on the role of a mentor as he is beginning to learn the trade. He has seen the end results of people doing the job correctly versus others who have miscalculated or attempted short cuts. Tapping into the knowledge he has gleaned from that show, along with watching YouTube videos, he has been able to build his own forge. He has become quite good at creating original pieces ranging in size from jewelry to iron gates. One of the most important details was building the forge in a way that the burning embers would get the airflow needed to fan them into fame and increase the temperature of the fire. If the forge can't get hot enough, nothing of lasting value can be produced.

In a similar way, we are built like a forge, and it's our faith that actively fans the flame of the Holy Spirit's fire in us so that we don't remain unproductive. The combination of our faith, and having trustworthy mentors like Paul in our lives to encourage us in our spiritual gifting, is imperative.

Paul continues in verse 7 to caution Timothy against a common downfall that plagues many of us...fear and intimidation. "For God has not given us a spirit of fear and timidity, but of power, love, and self-discipline." Timothy was to be fearless and bold before men, knowing that God would keep filling him with the power, love, and self-control that would be necessary for the job.

God's heart for you is that you would live by faith—a faith that fans into flames the special gift given to you. You are not to be fearful or feel alone. Pray and ask God to provide a mentor who understands your spiritual gifting, someone who will confirm and support you as you walk in that anointing. Your specific gift is meant to affect the lives of those God places within your circle of influence and your church family. Since that gift flows from the Holy Spirit dwelling in you, it will never be lacking in purpose.

Whatever gifting you have been given, it's not meant to be folded up like an extra special towel that is put away on a high shelf and out of your reach. Why would the Holy Spirit choose to give it to you, if you are not supposed to be using it? Life is messy because of the curse of sin in this world, and muddy boots abound. Be prepared and fearlessly ready in all seasons to bring out your towel.

Reflection: Am I walking fearlessly in the *dunamis* power and authority of the gifting the Holy Spirit has given me?

Meditation music: Fearless (in Your presence) or Spirit of the Living God

22.

Maintain the Light

In our cozy little country church, we have a prayer group that meets every Sunday morning. I remember one particular morning when a lady remained unusually quiet. Finally, she spoke up and said that while everyone was praying for the church, she could see a picture of a beautiful lighthouse on a hill. Beams of light were shining through the windows. The light that was pouring out was getting more brilliant as she watched. It was our church; we were being transformed into God's lighthouse on the hill.

John 8:12 tells us that Jesus said, "I am the light of the world. Whoever follows me will never walk in darkness, but will have the light of life." Within the Christian community, the lighthouse has become symbolic of Christ. Jesus said that He is the light. It's His light that shines brightly to bring in people who are lost or struggling through the storms of life. Many churches have used the concept of being a lighthouse because of the great interest and popularity of these nostalgic, historical buildings. Many people are drawn to these churches just because the picture portrayed gives them a warm, fuzzy feeling.

I admit that I have been caught up in the lighthouse fascination, along with millions of others who have taken vacations to go see them. A lot of people have beautiful, expensive collections of light-houses that they treasure. My inventory includes a few framed pic-tures, a coffee mug, and a few books of lighthouse stories. Nothing in my collection has much value, and it wouldn't interest anyone else, except maybe the books. Reading the stories helped me to picture the life of those who have been lighthouse keepers, their work, and the sacrifices they made in behalf of their calling.

At the beginning of this New Year, our pastor had an excel-lent message and shared a vision for our church. He challenged us to begin praying for God to bring new people into our church family. So, we started to pray for those who may come someday—including neighbors, friends, and others who don't attend any church. There has been a goal set to help keep us focused. For the past few weeks, we have kept the faith, prayed often, and remained very hopeful. Watching and waiting, on Sunday morn-ings we comfortably sit back in our pew and anticipate how God will move and make it all happen. After all, He is a Mighty God, and we are confident that He can do it all by Himself.

This week, I was studying in the book of Hebrews and came across a verse that really caught my attention. Hebrews 4:2 says, "For we also have had the gospel preached to us, just as they did; but the message they heard was of *no value* to them, because those who heard did not *combine it with faith*." As I mulled over this verse, I thought of the times when I have listened to an inspiring sermon, but after a few days I could only remember that it was memorable. Until someone else started talking about the actual points of the message, all I could do was agree that it was great.

What caused my memory to fail while someone else had it on the tip on their tongue? I don't think it had to do with my intelli-gence or lack of, but it had more to do with the truth that I discov-ered in this verse. The message was of *no value* to me, because I did not *combine it with faith.* I didn't combine the message with my personal faith and apply it in my life when I heard it. Therefore, it remained dormant because I remained unmoved.

Faith is a familiar word, but what is it? According to the Hayford Bible Handbook, faith is a belief in, or confident attitude toward God, involving commitment to His will for one's life. Faith is the essence of the believer's life from beginning to end.

According to the Bible, Abraham was a man of great faith. When God told him to leave his country and go to the land that He would show him, he listened, believed, and followed through with the plan. Abraham was committed and didn't put the idea on a back burner to simmer while he sat back comfortably on his pew and just prayed about the huge job of packing up his vast possessions, livestock, and family. When God pointed out the way to go, Abraham got busy with the task and went. Otherwise, God might have given Abraham's blessing of becoming a great nation to someone else who had an *active faith,* who was willing to work, press ahead, and move toward the vision.

In the New Testament, the apostle Paul encourages us in our faith as we read his charge to Timothy. "But you, man of God, *flee* from all this, and *pursue* righteousness, godliness, faith, love, endurance and gentleness. *Fight* the good fight of the faith. *Take hold* of the eternal life to which you were called when you made your good confession in the presence of many witnesses." 2 Timothy 8:11-12

The words Paul uses are active and forceful words to describe our Christian life. We are to flee, pursue, fight, and take hold. Living out our faith is not a passive state of inactivity, of comfortably sitting in our seat, while we wait on God to act. We can trust that God will indeed have His way when He is ready, but meanwhile, we need to press in, move ahead, and begin working.

Many pastors have wonderful messages, but they have *no value* to the church body if the people don't *combine them with faith*, an *active faith* that flees, pursues, fights, and takes hold of the vision. The picture of our church, or any other church, as being a lighthouse on a hill will only become a reality when we take hold of our role as lighthouse keepers.

We must understand that we are all called to be keepers of the Light... the Light being Christ. It's not a title for just the pastor or a few leaders, but for all of us who are believers and carry the source– Christ. When we gave our hearts to Jesus, He took up residence in us and began to radiate His beam through our lives. He fortified us with the Holy Spirit to give us the fuel and energy to shine effectively. But we have to work hard just like the lighthouse keepers in my books, who daily had to keep the gas beacon lit, clean the reflecting mirrors, and remove the soot from the tower windows. Individually, we must inspect the light shining from our own lives. The light of Christ never changes, so if it has dimmed, get scrubbing.

Is the light that radiates from our church sufficient to break through the fog and darkness that surrounds those who may be struggling or lost? If new people find their way here, will they have to be satisfied with a warm fuzzy feeling because we portray ourselves as a lighthouse? Or will they find us authentic and see the light of Jesus shining through us by our loving-kindness toward them? Are we truly being transformed into God's lighthouse on the hill with enough faith to do whatever it takes to maintain the Light?

There's a call comes ringing o'er the restless wave,
Send the Light! Send the Light!
There are souls to rescue, there are souls to save,
Send the light! Send the light!"

LET'S TALK ~ GOD'S HEART FOR YOU

We have a beautiful fluffy, white-taffy colored dog who spends his morning laying on the shag carpet near the bathroom door. He's a mix of Shih Tzu-Lhasa Apso and has the features and temperament of the latter, whose origins were in Tibet where the breed was highly regarded as excellent watch dogs in palaces and monasteries. In our house, he guards the royal bathroom. No one can quietly slip past Mercy to go in there without him. Most of the time if someone heads in that direction, he runs in before they can get there. But when you go in, he's nowhere to be seen. If you search, you will find him behind the shower curtain staring at the tile wall, wagging his tail so hard that his whole butt moves.

The morning sunlight shines brightly through the two windows in that bathroom. If you are wearing a watch, there is always a reflection that beams a spot of bright light that hits inside the shower. Mercy's morning quest is not to protect us or the bathroom, but it is to chase that light that bounces on the wall. It's really an obsession with him, and this habit is the highlight of his existence. Since I am the one who is home most mornings, Mercy regards me as the keeper of the light. He expects me to maintain the light. So I've put a small mirror on the windowsill so if there's sunshine, Mercy won't be disappointed.

In John 8:12, Jesus said, "I am the light of the world. Whoever follows me will never walk in darkness, but will have the light of life." Jesus is the light, and when we follow Christ, then we carry His light. That explains why Jesus and believers are both referred to in Scripture as being the light of the world. He dwells in us through the Holy Spirit, making it possible for us to reflect His character, like the mirror on my bathroom windowsill reflects a bright sunbeam to brighten Mercy's life.

Christians are to be filled with the attributes of the Spirit as described in Galatians in order to brighten the lives of others. Galatians 5:22-23 says, "But the fruit of the Spirit is love, joy, peace, forbearance, kindness, goodness, faithfulness, gentleness, and self-control." These attributes should be flowing out of our lives in a supernatural abundance that is capable of dispelling darkness. At times, my sister-in-law Jayne has struggled with the winter 'lack of light' syndrome. It's actually called S.A.D.-Seasonal Affective Disorder. Although she has learned how to alleviate it with brighter lighting and keeping active, what has made the biggest difference is that she has grown deeper in her relationship with the Lord. She starts her day with the Bible, devotions and prayer. Her source of Light—Jesus—is beaming from her life as she talks with people, writes inspirational posts on social media, and as she creates handmade gifts as surprise blessings to give away. She beautifully glows with unconditional love for others. She inspires me, as I see the fruit of the Spirit abound in her life. The light of Christ in us is meant to shine on people as if we were a city on a hilltop that can't be hidden. Matthew 5:14 (NLT) says that "You are the light of the world—like a city on a hilltop that cannot be hidden.

God's Heart for you is that you would be like a lighthouse on a cliff that towers over the vast sea of lost ships—lost people who are desperately searching for a little beam of hope. They may never be drawn to a church building, but God wants them to feel drawn to you. And when they look at you, they need to see the light of Jesus, a reflection of the Son shining through the windows of your heart and actions. When God stirs up an active faith within you, He will provide wisdom and direction as you minister to people around you, not only on Sunday mornings, but in your everyday life. Be diligent as you pursue a lifestyle of righteousness, godliness, faith, love, endurance and gentleness. Then you will be prepared for every situation and work that God has planned in advance for you to do. You will be blessed by God to be a blessing to others, filled with an endless source of hope to share. You will be a city on a hilltop who shines forth God's brilliance as you do whatever it takes to faithfully maintain the Light.

Reflection: Am I actively maintaining the Light of Jesus within me, so I can shine forth His love and hope to people He's placed in my life?

Meditation music: Way Maker or Send the Light

23.

Surrender

Sunday afternoon naps, as I fondly remember them, have become a thing of the past. For the last few years, when at all possible, I have tried to squeeze in at least a short one. Some people may believe naps are for the very young or the very old, but I have expertly justified my need for one—the adrenaline drain syndrome. From the moment that my alarm rings on Sunday mornings, I jump out of bed and into a routine requiring an adrenaline rush. There's a lot of hustling to be at church on time for the early morning praise team music run-through, and the sound checks. Then it takes a fair amount of energy to be alert and ready to play music on que during the church service. By Sunday afternoon, I'm yawning.

To be perfectly honest, I *have* gone to my quiet bedroom for the past few Sundays. If you were to open the door and peek in, you would assume that I was enjoying my same old traditional nap. But appearances can be deceiving. I can't remember the last time that God actually let me sleep. As I yearn for a deeper walk with

Him, my quiet time is no longer my own. It's another step of the ongoing work of the Holy Spirit, teaching me to surrender my will to His. It's not that I don't want to give God His way, but sometimes I don't understand what issue or attitude that I am hanging on to needs changed. According to the Bible, surrendering all things to God opens the door for him to continue his work in us.

In Romans 12:1-2, Paul writes to the Christians in Rome and believers everywhere, "Therefore, I urge you, brothers and sisters, in view of God's mercy, to offer your bodies as a living sacrifice, holy and pleasing to God—this is your true and proper worship. Do not conform to the pattern of this world, but be transformed by the renewing of your mind. Then you will be able to test and approve what God's will is—his good, pleasing and perfect will."

Paul urges us to offer our bodies (surrender them) to God as a living and holy sacrifice. Sacrifice of a living thing (animal) in the Old Testament always meant death, a bleeding out, a cutting apart, and then it was placed in the fire. In the New testament, God gave the life of His Son to suffer as the sacrificial Lamb in our place. The word Paul speaks has to do with a living sacrifice of our own desires. It is a death to our wants and preferences; it can be quite a painful struggle. God's desire to do a transforming work in us renews our minds, and brings a spiritual freshness beyond what we've experienced.

In Isaiah 49:16 (NASB) God said, "Behold, I have inscribed you on the palms of My hands; Your walls are continually before Me." My walls (my life) are spread out before the Lord. He sees it all, even some of the unfinished pages of the past. That Sunday afternoon, as I laid on my bed trying to nap, God picked up a pen. It was time for us to write the last few lines to my past history, so we could turn that old page once and for all. The issue that we had been dealing with during the week was unforgiveness. Being merciful, forgiving, and shrugging off most offenses aimed at me has usually been fairly easy for me to do. But I realized that if anyone has offended or has hurt someone I love, it causes a huge problem deep in my soul that I can't easily dismiss.

Last week, I had a phone call from someone that fits that profile. She happened to hear my bird whistling and she asked me about him. I said, "That's my cockatiel." She replied, "If you ever want to give him away, call me." I know that she loves birds and had 15 of them when she lived in Florida. The moment we hung up, my foot stomped in anger, and words flew out of my mouth rather loud and rudely, "She'd be the last person I'd ever give Tweeters to! Not after what she did!"

It was pretty obvious that I had a big problem, and God wasn't about to let it go unresolved. He said to me, "Give her the bird!" What? "Give your bird to her!" I was stunned speechless, and my heart was filled with turmoil. All evening I tried to ignore God's voice encouraging my heart to obey. Meanwhile, I was entertaining a taunting voice telling me I was justified in my unforgiveness. After a sleepless night of wrestling within my soul, by morning I knew what I had to do.

Although I have never had any intentions of giving away my beloved Tweeters, I had begun to feel sorry for him. He seemed so lonely lately. His friend, our parakeet, had died last spring. We go camping on most summer weekends, and he has been left home alone a lot. In my heart, I knew that this lady would take good care of him, and he would like being with other birds. Finally, I called her back, and she came to my house right away to pick him up. She was really happy and excited to see how beautiful he was. When she opened his cage, he flew to me, and held on with a death-grip. She had to pull him away from my shoulder, prying off each claw, one foot at a time. I felt like I was betraying him, which broke my heart. But I had surrendered my will to the Lord.

During the next few days, I really had the blues. My husband said, "Honey, we can get Tweeters back." He was very sweet, but I said, "No, God told me to give her my bird." You see, I had harbored a hardcore, defiant attitude of unforgiveness against her for many years. Most of the time it lay dormant, yet the issue was there just the same. It wasn't hidden from God. He saw it slowly growing moldy, musty and potentially dangerous in the basement of my heart. It needed to be exposed to the light, ASAP.

God knows my deep desire is to live my life in a manner that pleases Him. I want to understand God's ways and see everything through His eyes. That's driven by the Holy Spirit's transforming process in me. Unforgiveness was like a neglected, unruly hedge that was blocking the light of righteousness. It needed to be cut down and removed. Why wouldn't I expect it to hurt? Sometimes, our words of forgiveness to someone aren't enough, and God requires more. Our obedience is like a sacrificial offering that spiritually seals the deal, once and for all.

Sunday afternoon as I lay on that bed, I still had a few tears and I said, "Lord, why does it have to be so hard?" He loving said, "You had to give up your bird and send him away to complete the cycle of forgiveness; I had to give my Son. How do you think I felt?" John 3:16 "For God so loved the world that he gave his one and only Son, that whoever believes in Him shall not perish but have eternal life." God's sacrificial offering of Jesus Christ seals the deal for His salvation plan, and our redemption, once and for all.

LET'S TALK ~ GOD'S HEART FOR YOU

Think about your life—what are some of the things you have had to surrender? Do you remember how that made you feel? Was there a deep internal struggle against being submissive and giving up your control?

Most of us have surrendered our will in order to keep the peace with other people. It's a very different situation when God is calling and waiting for you to give up something that you have held close to your heart. Whether you are holding onto a good or bad thing, and whether it is a physical or spiritual issue, it could be the stumbling block that is keeping you from moving forward in the abundant life God planned for you.

Spiritual surrender is submitting your will to God's will. Being obedient is the key that opens the door for you to be able hear and discern the voice of God. When you are able to gather all the segments of what He is speaking to you, then you will have insight and a better understanding of where God is leading you.

Over the weekend, my husband and I were able to go to our home church. Three or four Sundays out of the month, we lead church services for other congregations. When we have a chance to sit back and be refreshed, God always touches us in a special way. Often, I have felt His presence provoking me in a good way to open up the box of my perceived, limited boundaries that I have unintentionally placed around Him. God was about to break down those ridiculous walls and expand my thoughts. What if God spoke the word 'surrender' and took us in a different direction than we expected? That's what happened to me so let me share this story.

On Friday morning, I opened my computer to write this Let's Talk wrap up section. I wrote a few paragraphs and waited for inspiration to come, but the Holy Spirit must have put my phone call on hold. I didn't get any response from Him, so I closed the computer. Sunday came, and when I least expected it the Holy Spirit came back on the line and began speaking to me. I was worshipping God in church with my eyes closed when unspeakable joy began to flow from my heart while singing the words, "There's power in the mighty name of Jesus; every war He wages He will win; I'm not backing down from any giant; cause I know how this story ends." This spoke to my heart that God already knows how each of my personal stories will end whether I submit to His will or not. And when I surrender to His will, it will end for His good purpose, and the enemy giant will never be able to use me for his evil plan.

The Lord spoke a word to our pastor to share with us. The word was, "Surrender..." Pausing for a moment to let us think about it, our pastor said the word slowly again and then expanded on what the Lord had said, "Surrender to the goodness of God." She had my full attention at the first word. I knew that I was hearing from the Lord concerning this devotional. While she was talking, one of our church elders came up and asked for permission to share some words the Lord had put on her heart for us. She had been on an airplane that was flying above very dark and gloomy clouds that were filled with rain. As she was looking at them, suddenly rays of sunlight burst forth and were ready to break through any opening in the cloud cover. As she sat in awe of the beautiful brilliance, the Lord spoke to her heart and simply said, "My ways are higher than your ways." Immediately, I remembered Isaiah 55:8-9 which says, "For my thoughts are not your thoughts, neither are your ways my ways," declares the Lord. "As the heavens are higher than the earth, so are my ways higher than your ways and my thoughts than your thoughts."

Next, our lead pastor challenged us to think about what it means to 'surrender to the goodness of God' in our own lives. He encouraged us to focus on it and see what God would show us through it. Then he shared his Thanksgiving message which expressed the importance of the songs of thanksgiving throughout the Bible. He explained about the supernatural power that flowed from an offering of praise and worship. Battles were won, God's people were released from captivity, temple ruins were restored, and city walls were rebuilt, all under the protection of the Lord.

I knew that God was connecting the story of my struggle of surrender to this new insight. "Surrender to the goodness of God; His thoughts and His ways are higher than your ways." Simply believe, trust, and sing your songs of thanksgiving throughout everything that is going on in your life, good or bad. Know that God is good all the time. In His timing, you will see the favor of God bursting forth like brilliant rays of sunshine. The gloomy rain clouds will begin to part as you look up to catch a glimpse of heaven breaking through your circumstances. Perhaps the Shekinah glory of God will fall. Surrender could be awesome! Just saying, what if...

Reflection: Am I willing to surrender all things by trusting in the goodness of God and knowing His ways and thoughts are higher than mine?

Meditation music: See a Victory or I Surrender All

24.

This morning throughout our church service, the Lord kept whispering to me. "Walk with Me, walk with Me, come away from the busyness of your day and the busyness of your mind. Walk with Me, come away from your doubts, fears, ambitions and desires. Simply, walk with Me."

About a month ago, the Lord had begun to urge me to fast and pray. He kept invading my thoughts with the same message, day after day. It didn't sound like much fun, so I didn't jump on the bandwagon right away. But late one evening, the Lord said rather sternly to me, "Fast and pray. Every time that you say no to food, you are saying yes to Me in obedience." Over this past year, God has been relentlessly teaching me to trust and obey Him. I am determined to be obedient, so I began fasting and praying every day and found that as I was drawing nearer to God, everything else was losing its importance in my life. Knowing that I was walking in obedience to my Father's will was sweeter than anything else could ever be. Psalm 119:103 says, "How sweet are your words to my taste, sweeter than honey to my mouth!"

Most days I have only been eating supper and then fruit at night. Yesterday was very difficult for me. I was feeling discouraged and vulnerable. As the day went on, I was hungry, and I began to see myself as deprived. I had been wanting a bagel for weeks. About mid-afternoon I caved in and toasted one, which I spread with scrumptious strawberry cream cheese. A little while later, my husband brought home a maple-iced cinnamon roll for me and laid it on the counter. I could smell the maple every time I walked past it. I would look at it and tell myself, "No." Then I would look at it again, and before long a little voice was starting to convince me that it would be ok to taste. It was telling me that I had already messed up my fast, so what would be the difference...it was only one little sweet roll.

Well, I still didn't touch it for hours. But later, while I fixed supper, I made myself a cup of coffee and reached over and took just a pinch of it. Then I nibbled little bites of it until it was half gone. The guiltiness over my disturbing weak will-power caused me to feel extremely unworthy of God's faith in me. Why in the world did He bother with me when I failed Him so easily. I could stand strong if a carrot tried to call my name, but I collapsed under the call of this pastry. What a pushover I'd turned out to be. When push came to shove in my resolve to fast, I tumbled.

I realize now that my irresistible attack of temptation was not just me battling with myself, but it was being made worse by Satan's taunting. He absolutely abhors my walk of obedience. The attack didn't stop there, either. The devil began to place doubts in my mind about the things that God had been showing and teaching me. When my will-power cracked under pressure, the enemy stuck a wedge in it and kept hammering it in deeper and deeper as I gave way to the temptation, one little nibble at a time. That's how the enemy sneaks in and slowly infiltrates in an attempt to ruin the progress God has made in our spiritual growth. And anytime he thinks he is succeeding; he will push us one step further toward our own self-destruction. He uses our insecurity, past failures, and self-doubt when we are in a weakened state of mind.

But God, in His loving way, reminded me that all is not lost when I mess up. He knows that the intention of my heart is to walk within the parameters of His will for my life. God reminded me about another word He had spoken to me: "Don't meander." Meander means a winding course, a bend in a road, a labyrinth, to wind about, a maze. This described what happened yesterday. Once I began to meander from the course God had set me on, Satan took advantage, and I was caught up in his maze. I took one wrong path, which led me on a never-ending bunny trail. I didn't find my way out until this morning when God began whispering "Walk with Me, walk with Me, come away from the busyness of your day, the busyness of your mind. Walk with Me, come away from your doubts, fears, ambitions and desires. Simply, walk with Me."

As I searched through the Bible to see if the actual words "walk with me" were in there, I found them in Revelations 3:4. It says, "Yet you have a few people in Sardis who have not soiled their clothes. They will *walk with me*, dressed in white for they are worthy." The church at Sardis was infested with sin and they were being urged to obey the truth they had heard when they first believed in Christ. There were only a faithful few who had remained obedient, and God said "they will *walk with me*, dressed in white for they are worthy."

They weren't worthy because they were perfect and never made mistakes. No doubt, they probably had days when they might have been tempted to take a step on the wrong path. But they didn't intentionally sin out of a rebellious spirit. Their hearts longed to follow Jesus. Therefore, they were made pure because of the righteousness of Christ that covered them. When our hearts long to obey the Lord, God sees us dressed in white, and He calls us worthy.

When I realized I had been meandering, I prayed for God to help me get back on track. I wanted to obey Him, even in a difficult fast, until He released me from it. I've always had a tendency to wander off when I became distracted, which would usually lead me down an unnecessary cul-de-sac. It would eventually loop around and take me back to the Lord, but I missed out on precious time that I could have spent with Him. When we walk with God, we are blessed as we trust and obey. Psalm 119;1-3says, "Blessed are they whose ways are blameless, who walk according to the law of the Lord. Blessed are they who keep his statutes and seek him with all their heart. They do nothing wrong; they walk in his ways."

"When we walk with the Lord, in the light of his word,
what a glory he sheds on our way!
While we do his good will, he abides with us still,
and with all who will trust and obey."

LET'S TALK ~ GOD'S HEART FOR YOU

Years ago, when my son Todd was a young teenager, we took a two-hour trip to Kinzua Dam. We invited my mother-in-law to go also. Well, Grandma Leila and her grandson sat in the back seat and they carried on with every breath they breathed, all the way there. Playfully picking and poking at each other, joking and laughing, sometimes they sounded like a couple of five-year-olds. Finally, my husband and I had enough of their boisterous, noisy behavior, and we warned them that they had to be on their best behavior on the way home or else! So, they sang silly songs all the way home, repeatedly throwing in the chorus of one of grandma's favorite old hymns, 'Trust and Obey.' There was nothing sweet and soothing about their rendition of it; it was belted out like they were a couple of 'out of control' sailors on a weekend pass. "Trust and obey, for there's no other way; To be happy in Jesus, but to trust and obey."After many years, those words still haunt me, but in a good way. It was a funny memory, and I admit that every once in a while, through the years, when grandma and my son reminisce and start singing that chorus again, we all have chuckled. I'm sure that all four of us have those words tattooed on a path in our brains from that trip. Maybe that's why we all have tried to be faithful to trust and obey the Lord throughout our lives.

At those times when obedience seems really difficult, look at it as a sacrifice that you are offering to God. It pleases Him, and often we are blessed in unexpected ways. I wrote a short reflection about this extended period of time of serious fasting that the Lord required of me.

My Secret Garden: *Fasting and prayer certainly isn't the easiest thing I've ever done. But I knew without a doubt that God was calling me to do it. Right away, I noticed that the more time I spent in prayer with God, the more time I wanted to be with Him. His voice became easier to recognize and everything I read in the Bible became magnified. I have been able to understand Scripture connections that I had overlooked before. I have found myself meditating on God's Word constantly, and often I have been tuning out the other people in our home. That wasn't necessarily always a good thing, because I'm pretty sure they sometimes felt neglected when they talked to me and I didn't respond right away.*

Fasting isn't easy. One Sunday after church, I felt famished. I made my husband, who was watching football, an omelet oozing with melted cheese and ham. I wanted to take one bite so bad that when I carried it in to him, there were tears dripping down my face. I went back to the kitchen to get a cup of coffee with the intentions of sitting beside him, looking like a saint in starving self-denial, while he tried to enjoy eating his food. But, as soon as I had my coffee ready, the Lord said, "Come away with me, walk with me. Let's go to your office." So, I went with Him and wrote this story, Walk with Me. That time we spent together held no comparison to that plate of forgotten lunch.

The experience of fasting and prayer is all about having a relationship. The Lord has pressed upon my heart that He has called me into an intimate dance. There's a song called, 'Dance with Me' that awakens my soul to long for our moments together. It's based on Song of Solomon 2:8, which says, "Listen! My beloved! Look! Here he comes, leaping across the mountains, bounding over the hills." You see, my beloved is eager to be with me. His love has captured my heart. As I go to my quiet place, I expectantly wait, for I know He will come. Winter is past and springtime has begun. I've entered through a gate to a secret garden that I'm not ready to leave. For the Gardener has much to show me and I am absolutely fascinated by the new hybrids that He's creating. There's a spectrum of color that takes my breath away, and hues of color within the experience of fasting and prayer that are indescribable. How can I ever leave the beauty that I've discovered here in this little piece of heaven with my Lord?

God's heart for you is to take this awesome key of fasting and prayer to unlock the gate of the Secret Garden that He has planted to share with you. He's prepared a special place that is not compromised by time and space, which is meant to delight your soul. It's a place for private encounters with Him, where you will join your hearts and hands together so you can walk through this life in the joy of His Presence. There is nothing more astounding than the realization of the greatness of His love for you. "I pray that out of his glorious riches he may strengthen you with power through his Spirit in your inner being, so that Christ may dwell in your hearts through faith. And I pray that you, being rooted and established in love, may have power, together with all the Lord's holy people, to grasp how wide and long and high and deep is the love of Christ, and to know this love that surpasses knowledge— that you may be filled to the measure of all the fullness of God." Amen. Ephesians 3:16-19

Reflection: Has the Lord captured your heart and brought you into His presence—an intimate 'garden' filled with His love, healing, and peace?

Meditation music: Not in a Hurry (United Pursuit) or Trust and Obey

25.

Layered Clay

Did you ever have a dream that seemed familiar? During the early morning hours in my sleep, I dreamed that I was attending a big dinner. I was mingling with friends beforehand, when a man and woman came over to me. He said hello, and then he introduced the woman as his friend. She stood solemnly still, never speaking, never really seeing me. They each wore a chain necklace with an amulet hanging on it. As they moved around the room chatting with other people, I knew that I knew him from somewhere. And I had an uneasy feeling.

Later in the lobby he singled me out and I said to him, "I know you; we sat together at the same table once before." He gave me a quizzical look, his eyebrows questioning, trying to figure out what I knew. I told him, "I know what you're up to."

I had watched him during the evening, talking to people, cornering each one alone. Then he would give them a small handful of clay that had a lot of thin layers. I watched them squeezing it and saw their faces becoming more fascinated as the beauty of the colorful layers took on a marbled effect. Soon the man would walk away smiling.

The same scenario continued to repeat itself over and over. At first, I thought maybe he kept the clay in that small container around his neck...but somehow, his supply never ran out. I began to suspect that he had laced the clay with drugs because of the unusual, strange, addictive effect that it had on those still clasping it. Was there a magic potion in the amulet?

Now face to face with this eerie man, he seemed to stare into my soul, as he slyly grinned and handed me layered clay. I knew that he would give me some and I had already planned how I would cleverly handle it. I had a Tupperware container with a lid! I would seal it in there. He couldn't outsmart me this time! We both knew what he was up to. Staring eye to eye, our hands met and he dropped the clay into mine. Quickly I reached toward the safety container to be rid of that putty. But my hand flexed, and it uncontrollably squeezed that lump.

How could my own hand deceive me so! How could I do what I knew I didn't want to do? I knew what was right so how could I falter so easily?

At that moment, I woke up and my arm was outstretched. My hand rested on top of my alarm clock right on the snooze button. Subconsciously, I had heard my alarm ring and had been automatically flexing my hand and shutting it off...every 9 minutes for an hour. How could I do that? When I went to bed last night, I planned ahead for my early morning, quiet time with God and set my clock. Nothing is more important to me than those moments, and I didn't want to miss it.

I'm reminded of Paul when he said in Romans 7:15, "I do not understand what I do. For what I want to do I do not do, but what I hate I do." I understand what he meant. I really hated that I turned off my alarm and didn't get up. It was never my intention to sleep in.

All Christians struggle against sin, and we must be careful not to underestimate its power. Satan is a crafty tempter and he knows every trick to get us to compromise our time and our walk with God. Another passage in the Bible says if your hand sins again you, cut it off. I'm not very happy with my hand turning off the alarm, but because of God's grace, I can keep my wayward limb. It's through His grace that I am forgiven-through the blood of Jesus. I can have victory over sin by the power of the Holy Spirit.

Another interesting aspect of the dream is that I recognized the woman. At first, I couldn't place her, but the face was familiar. She was a lady that I knew many years ago who was married and had bought a house nearby. She had adorable children and a husband that was always trying to please her. He worked overtime hours for extra income. He remodeled the house and built on a new bedroom. Often, they hired babysitters so they could go out together.

Soon after the remodel was finished, they sold the house and bought a newer, bigger one. But within a short time, she walked out on their marriage. Over the years, there were rumors of various boyfriends and more failed marriages. When I knew her, she had seemed so full of life. Now side by side with the man in my dreams, there was not even a glimmer of light in her eyes. Years of searching for something or someone to satisfy that humanly unquenchable need in her soul had drained her. Now she looked like the living dead.

My dream was a wake-up call to be aware of the ploys of Satan in my life. Even though I am a Christian, I am still vulnerable to his trickery. I know that I will still be like Paul and slip up and be unforgiving of myself and my foolish sins, but I hang on the promise in Lamentations 3:21-23 (KJV). "This I recall to my mind; therefore, I have hope. It is of the Lord's mercies that we are not consumed, because his compassions fail not. They are new every morning: great is thy faithfulness." His mercy makes it possible to live with ourselves when we have messed up. God's grace is sufficient.

Picturing that woman, I can't help but think of the people that I see every day whose eyes resemble her lifeless ones. They have resigned themselves to living their empty lives without hope. They don't know what it feels like to be cleansed by the blood of Christ and filled with the Holy Spirit. How desperate they must feel carrying a lifelong load of guilt, not ever experiencing God's mercy.

Through my dream, the Lord was showing me that the deceiver will always try to ruin Godly intentions with his schemes. But an even more crucial point is that God wants me to have a heart for people who don't understand that they are under the evil one's spell, mindlessly clasping his addictive layered clay. What once appeared marbled with veins of shaded beauty slowly became a muted gray-green mass of ugliness in their hands. They had accepted what they had been given, not questioning it anymore or wondering if life could be different. Gradually their eyes had dulled, covered over with hopelessness.

> Titus 3:3-7 says that "At one time we too were foolish, disobedient, deceived, and enslaved by all kinds of passions and pleasures. We lived in malice and envy, being hated and hating one another. But when the kindness and love of God our Savior appeared, he saved us, not because of righteous things we had done, but because of his mercy. He saved us through the washing of rebirth and renewal by the Holy Spirit, whom he poured out on us generously through Jesus Christ our Savior, so that, having been justified by his grace, we might become heirs having the hope of eternal life."

It's not a pretty picture that Scripture used to describe us before salvation. Shouldn't we who were once dead in our sins have a heart for those who are like the living dead? Father, stir up a passion in us to touch lost souls. Fill us with your Holy Spirit to empower us to help peel away the ugly layers of deceit from their hands, by the truth of your Word. Through your compassion and lovingkindness, help us to gently lead them to you, O God. Redeem and restore them to the abundant life You planned. Amen.

LET'S TALK ~ GOD'S HEART FOR YOU

I remember when my children were little and how much they loved playing with Play Doh or my homemade version of it. Of course, they had to sit at the kitchen table so I could keep an eye on them. I would tell them to be careful not to mix colors, although I knew they probably would. By the time they were done playing with it, there was always a pretty ugly glob that I had to pitch into the garbage. No sense keeping it because no one would want it the next time.

We're like those people in my dream, definitely including myself. We were handed temptation and we were not strong enough to resist engaging. My children couldn't resist their fascination to blend the colors even when they were warned. How often have you done something as an adult and later scolded yourself saying, "I should have known better!"

Romans 7:15: "I do not understand what I do. For what I want to do I do not do, but what I hate I do." Even Paul found himself frustrated with himself. Feeling frustrated with your sin is a good thing because it means that you are not ready to accept it as normal behavior. You are still tuned into the Holy Spirit who is trying to flush out all unrighteousness. He's sanctifying you. You are a work in progress that God watches over. And He stamps His approval over every step of the process. He never gives up on you!

In the Old Testament, dealing with our sin would have been a tedious process. If you have ever read the Book of Leviticus, which deals with purification requirements, you would only get through a few chapters before the word tedious would bombard your thoughts. To be cleansed from sin, you had to bring a perfect, flawless animal or bird for sacrifice to the temple. It was washed, then killed. Next, the priests had to cut and prepare it in very detailed, drawn-out steps in order for God to accept it.

Those of us living now are under the new covenant. According to the New Testament we only need to believe in Jesus, repent, and ask Him to forgive us. When we open our heart to Christ, our sins are covered by His righteous blood at the cross. The sin of our past, present, and future are covered under Jesus' sacrifice.

This is actually referred to as positional sanctification. At your time of salvation, you are completely forgiven. You are sanctified in the sight of God because of the work of Jesus. This goes hand in hand with justification. Because of Christ's atonement for our sin, God sees us as though we were perfect.

Practical sanctification is how we actually live day to day. The Bible talks about spiritual growth. We should progress from spiritual babes, feeding on milk, to spiritual maturity and desiring the meat of the Word. If we are content to remain as newly born-again babes, we will make a motley mess of the temptations or opportunities handed to us. Much of it will need to be tossed away. In other words, you'll stay like a little one trying to walk. Every time you take few steps, you'll fall. Even if you try again and again, you won't make much progress on your own. But If you reach both arms up for God to hold your hands, He'll teach you to walk. That intimacy grows you up. It strengthens your spiritual legs. Studying His Word gives you wisdom, and praying keeps you balanced in the choices you make.

The more you mature spiritually, the less the evil, eerie man in the room will be able to trick or seduce you to slide into sinful thought patterns and behavior. He might not be able to steal your salvation, but he can rob you of the life God has planned for you. He will attempt to gradually glaze your eyes over like a cataract, clouding the lens of your vision so you believe a worldly, distorted view of life. As we spiritually mature, God will give us eyes to see those around us with clear vision. We will begin to see and have a heart for people that others ignore and pass by. My granddaughter is in Singapore and told us that her mission team was in a café for lunch. She saw an old man sitting alone at a small table with his head bowed, starring at his cup of tea.

The Lord started to tug at her heart to go over to his table. She hesitated but finally went over. She spoke to him, but he never raised his head or moved at all. He wouldn't acknowledge her. She knew he understood her, because they all understand English. She asked him how he was doing. She offered to buy him food. When he continued to sit perfectly still, she told him she'd like to pray for him. So, she prayed God's blessing over him. Still no response. She walked away and felt disappointed that she couldn't reach him.

Then, God let her know that she did exactly what He was asking. She 'saw' this downcast, hopeless man and she reached out to him.

Maybe he was an angel placed there to see if her eyes were open to God's heart and agenda. It makes me wonder if we have 'seen' or missed 'seeing' one who was sent to check our response.

God's heart for you is that you have eyes that 'see' people and compassion to reach out to them. Be willing to help them physically so they feel God's love. Then, share about Jesus. "And do not neglect doing good and sharing, for with such sacrifices God is pleased." Hebrews 13:16 (NASB) Always remember, when you sacrifice your comfort zone to open your heart to others, God is very pleased with you!

Reflection: Is my heart flowing with God's compassion for others—if not, why not?

Meditation music: Give Me Your Eyes or Rescue the Perishing

26.

Be Still and Know

In Alaska, there is a family who owns a huge 600-acre homestead. For many years, they have been sharing their lifestyle through a reality show. My husband and I enjoy watching the family which is trying to be self-sustaining, as much as possible. Most of the men and women hunt deer, bear, and small game. They fish for salmon, halibut, and all kinds of seafood delicacies. They raise chickens, cows, and tend to their bee hives. Twice a year they saddle up their horses for a cattle drive to the upper bay, where the cows can graze all summer. And they grow huge vegetable gardens so they can preserve enough food for the winter months.

Often the men have to rig up pulleys and use old fashioned lever methods to get themselves out of a jam or to make their workload easier. Of course, we always keep in mind that this reality show is probably dramatically enhanced with situations that are created to keep us interested in watching it. But most of the time, they are portrayed as honest, loving, wonderful people who work from sunrise to sunset to live a more old-fashioned, wholesome lifestyle.

During the past few seasons, two of the adult grandsons have suffered life-threatening injuries. Through those difficult times, I have prayed for them as if they were my long-time neighbors. No doubt, they had many fans who prayed. But in all the programs that featured their journey of recovery, I don't remember any mention of God. Only during their Thanksgiving dinners has God been slightly, verbally honored.

This morning I have been thinking about the busy lifestyles we live. Are we so busy trying to be self-sustaining in the care of our family and selves that we rarely show our regard for God? While contemplating that thought, the Lord reminded me about the biography of Susanna Wesley and some of the stories that have been written about her. She was a devoted Christian who lived in the 17th century. Her father was a minister, and so was her husband. She had 19 children, but sadly, almost half of them passed away as infants.

Despite the tragedy of her loss, Susanna raised and homeschooled the rest of her children mostly on her own. Her husband often abandoned them for long periods of time as he traveled. For much of her life, she was solely responsible for sustaining her large family. Yet, amid the chaos of Susanna's over-burdened life, working from sunrise to sunset, there was one constant source of strength for her soul. Not a day went by that she didn't spend quiet time with God.

That sounds impossible with 10 active children, but it's true. Whenever she needed prayer time, she lifted her apron up over her head. The apron was a signal to the children to be quiet and to not disturb her. What a powerful reality show Susanna's life would have made. It could have been called, "Be Still and Know." Know what? That God was her comforter, strength-giver, provider, and the One her heart longed to be near. "Be still, and know that I am God! I will be honored by every nation. I will be honored throughout the world." Psalm 46:10 (NLT)

If I didn't know better, I would believe that this verse was tattooed on Susanna's heart. She yearned for Him. Her diligence in seeking God and in knowing that He was the life-blood that sustained her, was a seed that was sown into her children. It matured in the lives of John and Charles Wesley who became profound influences in the world of Christianity. Through their God-inspired theology and the hymn lyrics that were penned, we have all been blessed. John preached that salvation came through God's grace and having faith in Jesus Christ, not through the law or through church rituals. He preached in England and in America. Later he sent out missionaries to other countries. Charles wrote over 6,000 hymns which have not only glorified God, but they have encouraged Christians in their faith. Through the dedication of the Wesley family, God has been honored and exalted in every nation throughout the world.

The Alaskan frontier family produced a harvest of vegetable and meat that sustained them throughout difficult times. But eventually it was all devoured and forgotten as they worked to begin another cycle of the same self-sufficiency. Their story has been entertaining to a great many followers of their show for seasons. But someday, when their contract ends and the program is not renewed, the family and their achievements will be forgotten. Until their source of fame exalts the Lord, the eternal value of their public lives will be void of accomplishment for God's kingdom.

The Susanna Wesley family survived on the sufficiency of God's grace. Jesus said, "My grace is sufficient for you, for my power is made perfect in weakness..." 2 Corinthians 12:9. Through their reliance on God, an everlasting harvest of lost souls continues to be preserved forever in the kingdom. In the same way that, after a harvest, seed that falls from the mature crop into the fertile soil grows and produces more fruit. The work produced by the power of the Spirit continues on by the power of the Spirit.

If a reality show was produced about your life, what would it be called? My granddaughter Sierra's might be called, "Saved a wretch like me." I didn't make that up, it's what she has tattooed on the inner side of her arm. With her permission, I'm sharing a little of her story. She was a true child of God growing up, who in her early teen years had secretly endured peer pressure, bullying, and some abusive situations that were unknown to her family. Out of her need for self-preservation, she began to bully those who had been attacking her. In her desperation, she welcomed an ungodly spirit of rebellion because it brought her strength to fight those who had wounded her. In her young innocence, she didn't realize that same powerful spirit would turn on her and attempt to destroy her life. That full-on attack of the evil one drove her to destructive behavior for about a year. During that time, she had a huge knife tattooed on her upper arm. The image of that weapon was like Satan laughing in the face of God and proclaiming death over her life and her future.

But the spiritual battle for her soul was not to be won by the enemy, for she already belonged to God. The war was brutal, but nothing redeemed by God can be fully devoured by the enemy. Satan's stronghold was broken, nevertheless his teeth left scars on her. Jesus understood her pain and regrets. He pulled her back into His loving arms and restored her heart and soul.

The enemy of our soul is in a constant battle to steal our attention away from God. He wants to rob us of the power we have as believers in Christ. We have the choice to depend on our own strength and abilities and be earthly focused or to depend on God's strength and power and be heavenly focused. Only when God motivates our heart and soul can we overcome our struggles so we can live out His plan for us.

There's a new tattoo of a cross on my granddaughter's leg, for she has been raised from spiritual death and has been resurrected with Christ. The seed planted in her as a child went dormant for a season, only to spring back, filled with a faith that relies on the sufficiency of God. The Lord of the harvest will reap abundantly through her as she trusts in Him.

The story of God's Amazing Grace is all over Sierra, literally— from a life-threatening 'knife' of death, to the 'cross' of redemption and to her victory song 'Saved a wretch like me.' As she walks out the destiny of His calling, which has involved traveling overseas to serve with a mission group in the Philippines, the name of Jesus Christ has been and will be glorified. In a two-week period of time, she helped to rescue fifteen young women from human trafficking. After escaping, they were brought into the safety of an organization that provides a comforting, secure place for them to live and Biblical counseling to help restore their brokenness. In the future, the seeds planted from their testimony has the potential to bring other girls off of the dark streets of prostitution and into freedom found in Jesus Christ. Never underestimate the fruit of even one life redeemed by the Lord. "God will be honored in every nation. God will be honored throughout the world" Isaiah 46:10b.

Already, the Seed of the Spirit planted through Sierra's testimony has begun to bear fruit and produce a harvest of souls prepared for an eternity with God. It's a living legacy that will always point to the fame of our glorious Father. "For you have been born again, not of perishable seed, but of imperishable, through the living and enduring word of God. For people are like grass, and all their glory is like the flowers of the field, the grass withers and the flowers fall, but the Word of the Lord endures forever." ! Peter 1:23-25 May God be glorified!

LET'S TALK ~ GOD'S HEART FOR YOU

When people think about you and your life, what phrase, theme, or verse might come to their mind? Would they think about you as wonderful and entertaining like my Alaskan family, or would God's grace define you as it did in Susanna's legacy? Or would you fall somewhere in between and leave people wondering? If asked who in the Bible do you remind people of, who would they compare you to, or would your profile just blend into the mundane crowd?

Are you brave enough to be like King David who would open up his heart for God to examine? "Search me, God, and know my heart; test me and know my anxious thoughts. See if there is any offensive way in me, and lead me in the way everlasting." Psalm 139:23-24 What would God find tattooed on your heart?

Is the seed planted in you influencing the lives of people around you as John Wesley's did? The main message he preached was: Salvation comes through faith in Christ Jesus, not through the law or church rituals. The law protected us until we could be made right with God through His Son. It is by faith that we receive the promise of the Holy Spirit who dwells in us. It is by faith that we are blessed like Abraham to be a blessing to others.

Galatians 3:13-14,23,26,29

"Christ redeemed us from the curse of the law by becoming a curse for us...He redeemed us in order that the blessing given to Abraham might come to (us) the Gentiles through Christ Jesus, so that by faith we might receive the promise of the Spirit...Before the coming of this faith, we were held in custody under the law, locked up until the faith that was to come would be revealed... So, in Christ Jesus you are all children of God through faith...If you belong to Christ, you are Abraham's seed, and heirs according to the promise."

Therefore, we who belong to Christ are descendants of Abraham. We are inheritors of the promises God made to him. Abraham was blessed all the days of his life because he was empowered by faith as he vocally praised and honored God. "No unbelief or distrust made him (Abraham) waver concerning the promise of God, but he grew strong and was empowered by faith as he gave praise and glory to God, fully satisfied and assured that God was able and mighty to keep His word and to do what He had promised." Romans 4:20-21 (AMP)

Abraham never wavered in his faith. He walked in obedience to the Father's will. Abraham was confident that God was fully able and mighty to keep His word and promise. As we grow in faith, and are empowered by the Spirit, our lives will be Spirit led and Spirit motivated. We will clearly see that being self-sufficient is foolishness. When our lives are sustained by God, He will be our strength, provider, and protector.

God's promise to Abraham was "I will bless those who bless you, and I will curse him who curses you; and in you all the families of the earth shall be blessed." Genesis 12:3 (NKJV) Through our faith and obedience to God's will, all families of the earth will be blessed. How can that be? If we are a Godly influence in the lives of people around us, there's a domino effect. And it has the potential to trickle down through our generations of children.

We may never be able travel to other countries, but our prayers for the lost are powerful. By sharing from our financial blessing to support ministries, missionaries and those who travel on short term missions, like my granddaughter, nations will be blessed.

There's an endless, eternal harvest ripening if we will open our hearts for God to work.

In a hymn lyric that Charles Wesley wrote, he shared his heart-felt vision of the harvest of souls rejoicing.

"O for a thousand tongues to sing my great
Redeemer's praise,
The glories of my God and King, the triumphs of his grace.
My gracious Master and my God assist me to proclaim;
To spread through all the earth abroad the honors of
Thy Name."

Reflection: Am I faithfully carrying the blessing of Abraham to this generation? Is the seed of my life producing a harvest for the kingdom of God?

Meditation music: Amazing Grace (My Chains are Gone) or Amazing Grace

27.

Camouflaged Captivity

In the Old Testament, Zedekiah was made king of Judah by Nebuchadnezzar, the king of Babylon. He reigned in place of Jehoiachin. Neither he nor the people of the land paid any attention to the words the Lord had spoken through Jeremiah the prophet. King Zedekiah, however, sent a messenger to Jeremiah with this message: "Please pray to the Lord our God for us." Jeremiah 37:1-3

The king, officials, and the people of Israel didn't want to listen to Jeremiah's prophecies –the direct word of the Lord, but they wanted the blessings of his prayers. They desired what religion had to offer but not the cost. They were interested in what they could receive rather than seeking to establish or deepen their relationship with God. We wouldn't expect God to accept that shallow level of devotion from them, but what about from us?

Most Christians faithfully pray each day. That's a wonderful way to communicate with God, and it deepens our relationship with Him. But what is it that causes us to keep our prayer life so active? We might claim that we feel compelled to thank and praise Him for all that He has done in our lives. But is that the dominant reason why we pray? Could it be that we are driven by our desire to ask God to provide, protect, heal, and bless for our benefit? Are these needs the main draw that keeps us from skipping a day without this resource? Does this explain why reading God's Word, the direct Word of the Lord, often plays second fiddle to our daily habit of prayer?

There have been many times in my life that I have looked for my Bible on Sunday morning and found it still in my tote bag from my Tuesday morning Bible study. It shames me when that happens. I have often seen forgotten Bibles that people have left on the church pew for a week at a time. Didn't they miss them? Were they using a different Bible during the week or just not bothering to open any? Would any of us go from Sunday to Sunday without any prayer? Why does such an imbalance exist?

Lately, I have spent a lot of time studying about Israel's captivity in Babylon. They were not enslaved as their forefathers were in Egypt. Babylon's policy was to allow captives to settle in the land and live fairly normal lives. After many years, only the elders remembered the freedom they had in their own land. Except for the secondhand knowledge of the homeland, the children grew up not able to understand the significant differences. People actually built homes, planted crops, married, prospered, and families increased in number, according to Jeremiah 29:4-8.

After seventy years, Ezra 1:5 explains that when King Cyrus made a proclamation that all the exiles be released from captivity, only two out of twelve tribes left at that time. The other tribes were either so scattered or so comfortable in their lifestyles that they no longer yearned to move out of the land. Was their captivity so well camouflaged that they didn't recognize the areas in their lives that were still restrained and compromised?

Last spring when the stores were filled with summer clothes, I decided to take some of my young grandchildren to the store and let them pick out their own short sets. To make it extra special, I took them separately. We had a wonderful 'one on one' time together laughing and giggling at some of the outrageous fashions, wondering who on earth would actually wear them.

The clothes that they chose were fairly inexpensive, but I knew that those particular outfits would always be their favorites. Occasionally, they have been blessed with beautiful, designer name-brand clothing passed down to them from some older children at church. Although they are excited when they pull those costly fashions out of a bag, the fact remains that they are secondhand. They are wonderful to have but will never hold the same significance as the clothes they picked for themselves, 'one on one' with Grandma.

In a football game, the same principal applies with the fans and the players. Enthusiastic fans can be very elated or very sulky after watching their favorite team win or lose. Yet they are only spectators, experiencing the game secondhand. Only the players who have that 'one on one' physical involvement can understand the true depth of elation in winning a game or the depth of despair over losing one.

For most of my life as a Christian, I have been satisfied with a secondhand relationship with my Father when studying the Bible. There were years when I faithfully listened to Christian radio and TV programs and played recorded Bible study series. On a weekly basis, I attended Bible study groups and went to church. I was learning, growing, and walking fairly close to God. But for the most part, I relied on others to glean the Scripture and pass on their great spiritual insight to me. In my busy lifestyle, it was easier to keep doing my housework or driving the car, combining that task with listening to someone else teach me God's Word. It's not that it isn't a good thing to do, but it should only be a supplement.

In my life, other teachers were in the place that God wanted for Himself. My Father desired a 'one on one,' firsthand sharing time with me each day. Now as I open the Bible, He engraves words on my heart that touch specific emotions, attitudes, and strongholds that are unique in my life. He helps me to understand passages that have triggered release, healing, and hope. God continuously calls my heart into obedience to come into His throne room. Sometimes it seems like a challenge to set aside that time, but they have become the moments my heart longs for each day. Hearing my Father's voice and embracing His tenderness meant just for me, will always draw my heart. It brings the sweetest joy I've ever known in this life.

I've learned that when we neglect reading God's Word, the direct Word of the Lord, we aren't much different than King Zedekiah and the people of Israel. They sought after what God could do for them instead of seeking a relationship with Him. Are we like those ten tribes who, after they spent 70 years captive in Babylon, were satisfied to remain behind while the other two tribes packed and set off on their journey home?

Those who remained behind were comfortable in their fairly free lives. Hearing secondhand about the good life back in the homeland was enough to keep them content to stay awhile longer. Until they had significant reason to leave convenience behind, they refused to move forward to complete freedom. Didn't they realize that partial freedom was still captivity?

Often, excuses are not justifiable but are Satan's camouflage to hide truth. They let us remain comfortable living where we are spiritually content. We can't see God's vision for the relationship He desires to have with us. We are fooled to believe that we are in good shape. But secondhand knowledge and styles have no place in our backpack as we step forward to walk with God to unknown realms. Until we set off on the journey to experience first-hand that 'one on one' relationship with our Father, like Israel, we will continue to live mundanely in camouflaged captivity.

LET'S TALK ~ GOD'S HEART FOR YOU

As I was studying in the Book of Jeremiah this morning, it was interesting to find that one of the most commercialized Bible verses, Jeremiah 29:11, which has been printed on mugs, tee shirts, and on framed art, is in the same chapter that told about Israel's lifestyle as captives. Chapter 29 is the text of a letter of instruction and encouragement from the Lord, written by Jeremiah to those living in captivity in Babylon. They were told to settle in, build, plant crops, marry, and have families. In addition, they were told to pray for the peace and prosperity of Babylon. Then, they also would receive peace and their families would prosper there.

In the next section was God's promise that would lead many of them to seek the Lord. Jeremiah 29:10-14: "This is what the LORD says: 'When seventy years are completed for Babylon, I will come to you and fulfill my good promise to bring you back to this place. [11] For I know the plans I have for you,' declares the Lord, 'plans to prosper you and not to harm you, plans to give you hope and a future. [12] Then you will call on me and come and pray to me, and I will listen to you. [13] You will seek me and find me when you seek me with all your heart. [14] I will be found by you' declares the Lord, 'and will bring you back from captivity..."

God's heart for you is centered on the popular verse Jeremiah 29:11. His plans are to prosper you, give you hope, and a future. Who doesn't want to receive all of that from the Lord? Yet you need to read further and see that it is your responsibility to call on God, and pray; then He will listen. It is a conditional verse that requires spiritual commitment for God's plans for your life to be fulfilled. You are to seek Him with all of your heart–study His Word! He promises that you will find Him. Then God will bring you out of captivity–any struggle, stronghold, or misconception that has held you bound.

God knows all about the lifestyle that you are living. He understands your time-consuming responsibilities and busyness. The Lord knows that you love Him. He even knows who your most respected Bible teacher or preacher happens to be. He probably placed them in your life so that you would learn and grow. But God never wanted you to feel content to only experience Him on a second-hand basis.

God's heart for you has always been to be directly involved in a personal 'one on one' relationship with you. It's always been His desire to teach and speak to you directly, through Scripture and prayer, during your quiet-time together. His voice is full of tenderness and love. Your heavenly Father knows you better than anyone and knows the exact words that will minister to your heart and your needs. God will clearly guide you and help you make important life choices. Even if you are blessed to have spiritual leaders who have spoken encouragement and direction, God still wants to have the final say. Take those words and talk to God about them. Ask Him to confirm or alter them according to His will.

The Lord wants a firsthand relationship that includes filling you with His wisdom and knowledge. As your 'one on one' relationship with God matures, the influence of teachers and the encouragement from others will be like the nuts and cherry on the top of a hot fudge sundae. It's a wonderful embellishment but the sundae is deliciously satisfying without it. Nothing can compare to experiencing the fullness of our God.

1 Kings 8:23 (NASB) tells us "...There is no God like You in heaven above or on earth beneath, keeping covenant and showing loving-kindness to Your servants who walk before You with all their heart."

God is so full of loving-kindness for you. As you seek Him with all of your heart, He will hear you and draw near. You have His promise that the Lord Himself will oversee your growth and bring you to maturity. "...He who began a good work in you will carry it on to completion until the day of Christ Jesus." Philippians 1:6.

God will never give up on you or His blueprint for your life. The powerful name of Jesus has the power to break every chain that has kept you locked in camouflaged captivity. He will reveal the truth so that you can see more clearly and escape your mundane, convenient lifestyle. As you draw nearer, the Lord will work faithfully to move you into position to walk out the purpose He has destined for your life. "You will make known to me the path of life, in Your presence is fullness of joy, in Your right hand there are pleasures forevermore." Psalm 16:11 (NASB) Come into His throne room and experience the 'one on one' splendor of God's Presence for yourself. In that intimate relationship, you will find inner joy, strength, and wisdom to continue on a spectacular journey in this life, and as He eventually leads you back home...to heaven.

Reflection: Lord, I long to come closer to You. Show me if there's a camouflaged, invisible chain hindering me that needs broken by the power of Your name.

Meditation music: Break Every Chain or Victory in Jesus

28.

Thanksgiving

Thanksgiving Day will soon be here again, and once more, I'm reminded of my childhood. When I was growing up, we had a turkey dinner only once a year. The aroma of Thanksgiving Day was like no other. The smell of turkey roasting, fresh dinner rolls baking, and the smell from spicy pumpkin and apple pies covering the counters were more memorable than the meal itself.

I was reminded of those days as I read through Numbers 15. The word 'aroma' caught my eye because it was used over and over as the Lord was speaking to Moses. He was giving him detailed instructions for the Israelites to follow when they entered the land that He promised them. Most of the chapter deals with offerings and sacrifices. They are told which type of meat is to be brought, how to prepare their grain offering, and they were also told to bring a drink offering.

As these gifts were offered to God, the Scripture said that it was "an aroma pleasing to the Lord." The phrase, "an aroma pleasing to the Lord" was used six times. I thought about the smell of those things when put on the fire. Did God relish that aroma just as I remember those Thanksgiving Day smells? Or is there more being said than what meets the eye?

God began to remind me of something He spoke to my heart last Thanksgiving. It was the day before, and I was about to begin the task of baking pies. Before I started, I flipped the T.V. station to the Christian channel and caught a line from a song being sung, "We are to God an aroma of Christ." Immediately the words took root in my spirit.

All day I kept thinking about them. How can we be an aroma of Christ? It's not too difficult to be that to the people around us. Most of the time we can 'put on Christ' and be loving and kind, at least on the surface. Even when our hearts and attitudes are secretly grumbling, we can usually fool people if we try. But the song said "We are to God an aroma of Christ." As I wrapped my mind around that phrase, I realized that line brings us to higher level of accountability. God sees the heart and can never be fooled. Even if we strive sincerely to be that aroma of Christ to God, truly, it can only happen when our sinful nature is fully submerged and covered by the righteousness blood of Jesus. 2 Corinthians 2:15 tells us; "For we are to God the pleasing aroma of Christ among those who are being saved and those who are perishing."

God's timing is always so perfect. He planted those precious words of truth in my heart because He was preparing me for what was about to unfold the next day. On Thanksgiving Day, we went to our parent's house carrying the pies I had baked, ready to enjoy a wonderful time. As we walked into the kitchen, the aroma was just as sensational as I knew it would be. We put the pies on the counter and then we began to greet everyone as we went from room to room.

Before long, things began to heat up and stir and it wasn't just the food. There had been some past misunderstandings among my siblings, which had never been resolved. It caused some intense tension, which led them to avoid each other. People had deliberately scattered throughout the house, so they didn't have to talk to each other. In the living room, we had the opposite scenario happening. I heard too much talking going on when the subject of politics creeped into the conversation. Soon, strong emotion-filled opinions were being expressed, which brought even more uneasiness and division. It was becoming quite an ugly scene, and those of us working in the kitchen to finish the final prep for the Thanksgiving feast began to doubt if anyone would stay and eat. There was no thankful celebration happening at this house; the aroma had become like spoiled milk.

It's not unusual for turmoil to occur even in a Christian home, because the enemy is always in an attack mode, trying to divide families. What happened was no surprise to God. For a change, I wasn't part of the problem because God had grabbed a hold of my attention and I had listened to the leading of His Spirit. He had spent the previous day preparing my heart for that unnerving situation. Amid the strife, I recalled the Lord's Words. Over and over I silently repeated "I am to God an aroma of Christ."

It was very difficult to keep myself under that covering of Christ's righteousness. I wanted to be angry at those who were ruining my day, but instead I began interceding in prayer for them. Except for the Lord's deep-rooted presence in my heart, the aroma of that Thanksgiving Day was begging to be erased from my memory bank...every detail forgotten forever. But I can never forget God's mercy over our family, and the important lesson that He taught my heart during that holiday.

As I reread through Numbers 15, it became obvious that the "aroma pleasing to the Lord" was more than just an actual smell. It was all about the condition of their hearts. Did they bring their offerings with willing, thankful, repentant hearts?

When God looks at what I offer up to him daily, is my attitude and heart's condition an aroma pleasing to Him? And does He see any trace of Jesus in me? Have I made putting on Christ's attributes a conscious, deliberate effort each day? Is my spirit fully engaged in the righteousness of Christ, producing the spiritual fruit God expects?

In Philippians 1:9-10, the Apostle Paul wrote this encouragement to believers, "And this is my prayer: that your love may abound more and more in knowledge and depth of insight, so that you may be able to discern what is best and may be pure and blameless until the day of Christ, filled with the fruit of righteousness that comes through Jesus Christ–to the glory and praise of God." Amen.

LET'S TALK ~ GOD'S HEART FOR YOU

Have you ever spent a lot of time planning a vacation or a holiday celebration that seemed to backfire in your face? Through no fault of your own, everything that could possibly go wrong, did? Maybe you can relate to my Thanksgiving celebration that turned out to be more of a nightmare. Well, if you can't relate, just ask Jesus how that feels...

As I write this section, we are preparing for Palm Sunday and Easter. We celebrate now, but at the time, Jesus was about to encounter a real nightmare. Of all the terrible things to deal with, Jesus was about to face His own horrific death, through 'no fault of His own!' Meanwhile, no one else knew what was about to happen except His Father.

Matthew 21:8-9 tells us about the excitement of the people when Jesus entered Jerusalem riding on a donkey. "A very large crowd spread their cloaks on the road, while others cut branches from the trees and spread them on the road. The crowds that went ahead of him and those that followed shouted, 'Hosanna to the Son of David! Blessed is he who comes in the name of the Lord! Hosanna in the highest heaven!'"

The people of Israel were waving palm branches and celebrating! They thought Jesus was coming to be their new king and ruler. They thought that, finally, they would not have to suffer under the Roman rulers. The crowd was excited, and they were celebrating their coming freedom from persecution. Little did they realize it would all take a different turn than they expected. It would seem to backfire in their face.

For Jesus, He knew that the present celebration was premature, and He knew how it would all end. Through 'no fault of His own', everything that could possibly go wrong would, or so it would seem, because of the suffering He would soon face. As Holy week played out in real life and time, Jesus and the disciples gathered to celebrate the Passover. The aroma of that upper room should have been 'an aroma pleasing to God.' After all, the room was reserved for Jesus and His disciples, whom He had lived with and personally taught for three years. They were trained to be ministers of the Gospel.

Yet there was a disturbing smell seeping into the room, the odor of a coming betrayal and repeated denials that would soon play out, just as Jesus predicted. At the moment, there was also the stench of ridiculous bickering filling the room as the men sat around the table. "Then they began to argue among themselves about who would be the greatest among them." Luke 22:24 (NLT)

Oh, how merciful is the love of Jesus! It's hard to believe that His 'beloved' disciples could be vulnerable enough for that creepy enemy, Satan, to so easily mess with their hearts. How easy must it be for us to fall prey to the evil one, unless God intervenes and prepares us ahead of time. Scripture tells us, "Therefore, prepare your minds for action. Be sober-minded. Set your hope fully on the grace to be given you at the revelation of Jesus Christ." 1 Peter 1:13 (BSB) We are not to be caught off guard but we are to be alert at all times.

In this world we will always have turmoil, no matter what century or millennium we are living in. What my family experienced that Thanksgiving Day was 'nothing new under the sun' as the saying goes. Nothing that day was my fault. What truly happened was a spiritual battle caused by the devil to divide us from God's perfect plan for our family. What happened to Jesus was not because of any personal fault, but quite the contrary. Because His character was absolutely perfect, He was the only one to ever live in this world who could carry out God's perfect plan for salvation. It came through a grueling spiritual battle that Satan really thought he won on the day of Jesus' crucifixion.

But nothing was further from the truth. Victory belonged to God, even as His Son walked in obedience to be the sin sacrifice for the world...what 'a pleasing aroma of Christ' to His Father! From the stench of death to the fresh breath of Spring, Resurrection Day came and the celebration of Easter is forever in our hearts as we look forward to eternal life.

God's Heart for you is that you would be celebrating what Christ has done for you. Eternal life with Him is secure if you have been saved. Yet you will have to endure serious spiritual battles with Satan while you live on this earth. Allow God to prepare you in advance to face the unpredictable situations that you will face. God wants you to be sober-minded and ready to act according to the insight and wisdom that He already placed within you. You are not to be so shocked by surprise circumstances that you become stunned and unresponsive. You need to know the Word of God, and your spirit needs to abide in His Spirit. God expects you to be able to discern the spiritual atmosphere around you on all occasions. Then as a Christian, you will truly be "to God the pleasing aroma of Christ among those who are being saved and those who are perishing." 2 Corinthians 2:15

Reflection: Have I truly laid down my life so that I can be raised up with Christ and covered by His aroma, which is pleasing to God?

Meditation music: Once and for All or In Christ Alone

29.

The Snowman

"Do You Want to Build a Snowman?" That popular song from the Disney movie 'Frozen' has come to life this week, as schools have been closed because of the blustery snow and ice storms moving through our area. It's February in Pennsylvania! No doubt that lyrical line from the song was spoken between friends, brothers, and sisters. This snow came down heavy and had the perfect wet packing consistency needed to build the best snowmen. It made me wonder how long people have been building them.

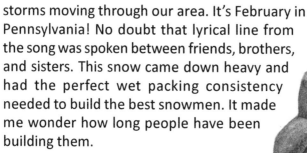

According to the 'Book of Hours', which is found in the National Royal Library in the Netherlands, there is an illustration of a snowman dating back to 1380. Perhaps people have always made them. Can you believe that there is actually a World Day of Snowmen celebrated on January 18th each year? The town of Bethel, Maine holds the Guinness world record for building the tallest snowman, that towered at 122 feet and weighed approximately 13 million pounds. I doubt if the children built that one!

Many times, when we were young, my brothers, sisters, and I wished and prayed for really bad snow storms to close our school. But the weather was never too bad for us to beg our mom to let us go outside and play in it. I remember my Mom lining us up in the kitchen and helping six of us put on layers of clothing. She would zip, snap, and button up our snowsuits, then tie the strings on our hoods. She'd tug up our boots and tightly hold our gloves as we wiggled each finger into the right opening. Finally, mom would finish us off by covering half our face with a wide scarf that was wrapped several times around our neck and tied. We were bundled so tightly we could hardly move, but we were warm enough to play for hours.

When our gloves became too wet or our boots leaked, Mom would warm up our hands and help us put on another dry pair of gloves. We didn't have extra boots, so we'd warm up our feet and put on a couple layers of dry socks. Finally, mom would put a long plastic bread bag over each foot, then we'd slip them back into the wet boots.

We lived in the country with a big yard and fields to play in. Surrounding our property were many acres, owned by my relatives, that had hills for sled riding and a pond for skating. But when our younger siblings came outside with us, we had to stay close to the house so our parents could help keep an eye on them through the windows. That's when we'd pair off and see who could build the best snowman. My older twin brothers always rolled the most massive snowballs, and their snowman always towered over the rest. My older brother and I couldn't build ours nearly as tall, so we'd give ours great details like a happy face, a scarf wrapped neck, stone buttons down his chest, and twig arms. In our vivid imaginations, I'm sure we thought our snowman looked like he was only a magic black hat away from coming to life, just like Frosty! When we were finished with ours, we all rallied around the little ones and helped them build their tiny snowman. Most of the time, Mom practically had to come outside and drag us into the house a few hours later. By then, we were getting tired and cold with snow clumped on our scarves, gloves, and anywhere it could cling to. Even though we were usually soaked from head to toe, we pouted, because we loved playing in the snow. But when the door opened into the kitchen, the wonderful aroma caused our tummies to growl with hunger pains, and we quickly changed our attitude. We could smell the pot of homemade hot chocolate warming on the stove and the cookie tray full of toasted cheese and toasted peanut butter sandwiches inside the oven that were almost ready to eat. Our Mom was the best! She faithfully provided for us in advance, as she anticipated our need for dry clothes and warm food for our little bellies. She was full of patience and lovingly took care of us.

Looking back now, I realize that God had provided a very blessed life for me growing up, even though my parents had to stretch every penny to buy the basic things we needed. God blessed us with a simple, country lifestyle, with parents whose life centered on their family. Growing up in our home, their loving care gave us a better understanding of God's heart and love for us. We knew we were loved whether we were being 'naughty or nice.' That love was unconditional.

Romans 5:8 tells us, "God demonstrates his own love for us in this: While we were still sinners, Christ died for us." Our Heavenly Father has a sacrificial love for us that is far deeper than the sacrificial love I received from my parents.

I love the passage in Isaiah that describes God's heart for us. Isaiah 49:15-16 says, "Can a mother forget the baby at her breast and have no compassion on the child she has borne? Though she may forget, I will not forget you! See, I have engraved you on the palms of my hands; your walls are ever before me." God is telling us that His compassion for us infinitely exceeds those of the tenderest parents toward their children. He writes our names on His hands so that He is always mindful of us.

Zephaniah 3:17 declares, "The Lord your God is with you, he is mighty to save. He will take great delight in you, he will quiet you with his love, he will rejoice over you with singing." Our Heavenly Father takes great delight in us. We are His beloved children whom He comforts with a lullaby of endless love. And God considers us to be His children no matter what age we happen to be, eight or eighty. We will never become too grown up or mature to be called by our Father to come in from the cold and be warmed by His arms. He anticipates our every need and provides in advance for times when life gets blustery or frigidly frightful. He is mighty to save us from pelting hailstorms in the winter seasons of our lives.

Throughout the future, children all over the world will continue to wish and pray for blizzards so school will be canceled. Many will call other neighborhood kids and ask, "Do you want to build a snowman?" Bundled warmly in their winter clothing, they'll join together to accomplish a fun adventure of bringing their imaginary snow friends to life. I'm guessing that most of us don't have friends who want to play in the snow anymore. Watching it through a window as it falls and covers everything with a beautiful, white, fluffy blanket, brings more pleasure than going outside and freezing.

Yet, something in my soul still longs to be able to have that enjoyment and comradery of a great friend to help build something unexpectedly magical like Frosty the snowman. My imagination begins to soar, knowing that, with God, all things are possible. It's in those special moments that I sense the Holy Spirit stirring my heart to answer His call, "Do you want to build a Kingdom?" As He leads me, I write my stories and share the Gospel in my testimony of God's grace, that is continually transforming my life. Through the inspiration of the Spirit, I am blessed to partner with

Him as I respond to His call. In whatever way He leads, I am to encourage His beloved children, which builds up the body of Christ, God's Kingdom.

LET'S TALK ~ GOD'S HEART FOR YOU

Listen up, children of God, has your phone been ringing? Have you been waiting for your normal, routine life to be interrupted by a snow blizzard or maybe an ice cream blizzard? Has your soul been longing to be satisfied by something more spectacular than either of those things? 2 Timothy 1:9 (BSB) tells us, "He has saved us and called us to a holy calling, not because of our works, but by His own purpose and by the grace He granted us in Christ Jesus before time eternal."

According to 2 Timothy, you were saved and were called to a "holy calling." Your soul is longing to powerfully move in the calling that the Holy Spirit has chosen for your life. Your spirit can only be fully satisfied when you are serving the Lord according to the purpose God planned for you. After you become a Christian, the Lord fills you with His Spirit so that you can partner with other believers to help build His Kingdom.

At the beginning of this story, I shared about the town of Bethel, Maine. It has the record for building the tallest snowman that was a towering 122 feet! For one man working alone, the task would have been impossible, but the whole community joined together to work and made the project possible. Their successful accomplishment came as a result of unity, combined with purpose. What's even more interesting to me is the fact that the town's name Bethel means House of God. I believe the Lord pointed me to this story so that I could to relate it to our church body. Working alone, much is impossible. When you join yourself with the power of the Holy Spirit, then anything is possible. But when a community of believers work together, led by the Spirit, wondrous marvels can unfold. Psalm 133:1 says, "How good and pleasant it is when God's people live together in unity!" We are the House of God. Spectacular things could be achieved to build up the Kingdom of God if we became more unified in His purposes.

In my own experience, when God gave me a vision for Hope House Ministries of Adonai, He already had in place a support team. I was never meant to do anything by myself. Together, there were a dozen of us who prayed for over a year before the ministry was activated to serve other people. God worked within our group to develop our faith and to teach us to minister to each other in the power of the Holy Spirit. Through prayer, He gave us a gift of discernment and a deeper insight into the spiritual realm so that we could better understand the struggles and battles that we all face in this life.

When God told me to write this book, He knew it was impossible for me to do it on my own. I wasn't a writer or journalist. But like a loving parent, God provided for me in advance before I knew of His plan. He gave me a network of family and friends to be encouragers, someone to edit, and another to illustrate the book. Throughout this whole impossible adventure, God has made it possible because of the body of Christ working together. We have been united in building His Kingdom through Hope House Ministries and this unexpected book.

God's heart for you is that you would open your spiritual eyes and ears for whatever He has prepared for you to do. Do not be fearful; you are not alone. Your Heavenly Father knows you more intimately than anyone else and even better than you know yourself. If God gives you a vision or an idea, then He will also surround you with the necessary support to make the impossible, possible. Your Father is a parent who anticipates your every need before you ask. He loves you more than the mother who nursed you as a baby. Your name is inscribed on the palms of His hands. There is no 'calling' that God plans for your life that is beyond the ability of the Holy Spirit to enable you to do. When you sense the Holy Spirit stirring your heart to answer the call, "Do you want to build a Kingdom?" you can trust that your Father knows that you are ready. So, bundle up in the layers of God's armor and move through the door He opens for you.

Revelations 3:8 says, "…I have placed before you an open door that no one can shut…" Go out in peace, and trust the Lord.

Reflection: What if the Lord began unlocking a new door for you to step through, which would require you to serve Him in ways that pushed you beyond your natural abilities? Would you be willing to trust Him?

Meditation music: Unstoppable God or We've a Story to Tell to the Nations

30.

Special Delivery

It's the most wonderful time of the year! The season of festivities has begun. People are full of cheer and excitement. Thanksgiving Day has drawn family and friends to gather together for a heartwarming time of not only sharing food but for sitting back and sharing our lives. It's so special as each person shares something that they are thankful for before we pray over the food. It's a sweet time for remembering the countless blessings that God has given us.

After hours of cooking, I'm also very grateful to have leftovers for the next day, because at midnight, the Black Friday rush officially begins. Being older and wiser, I sleep, while my daughter and granddaughters eagerly shop all night for bargains with my gift list and money. They love it, and so do I. After a full night of rest, no one has to tell me to be of good cheer. My heart is pretty happy as I grab my morning coffee and boot up the computer to find great deals shopping online.

This year, I even searched for Christmas cards on the internet. I found one with a beautiful snow scene that featured an open mailbox that was full of Christmas cards. Although it was a very simple design, it touched something deep inside me. It was nostalgic and reminded me of my childhood. You see, my dad worked at the post office while I was growing up. We were a family with eight kids, and when the Holiday season came, my dad was always excited for the opportunity to work a lot of overtime. He was a mail sorter, and thousands of colorful envelopes passed through his hands before they were delivered. Even though it was exhausting, he was thrilled to be able to afford a few gifts to put under the Christmas tree for each of us.

In those days, everyone sent Christmas cards. Most people spent hours writing them because each one carried a personalized message. Rarely did people type a family newsletter that was tucked into every card. Often, folks watched for the mail carrier to come each day. Even when I was growing up, I remember seeing my neighbors standing out by their mailboxes along our road, waiting. When the mail arrived each day, it was a special delivery that carried a lot of love and cheer.

Not too long ago, I came across a true story my Aunt Dorothy had written about her years growing up in the area now known as Lake Arthur or Moraine State Park. There was an old mining village called Isle, which now lies underwater at the bottom of the huge lake, near the Route 528 bridge. The town boasted of a big General store called Watson's. It was like a community center that was always bustling with shoppers, wiggly children, and probably the latest gossip. My Aunt Dorothy said that children were always treated with penny candy when they came into the store with their mothers. She remembered taking her candy stick outside, so she could ride on the big porch swing while she waited. Inside, retired gentlemen, miners, and farmers gathered on wooden benches by the old coal stove to keep warm, smoke their pipes, and share stories with their neighbors.

There were thirteen homes in the village; mostly miners, who earned about $2.50 a day, lived there. The Western Allegheny Railroad ran through the town and carried freight, feed and supplies to the store. The train also delivered appliances, furniture, and clothing that folks ordered from the Sears & Roebuck catalogue. Then the train, loaded full of coal, traveled on to Pittsburgh.

In the surrounding area, there were many farms and country homes. My grandfather was the mail carrier for most of his life in that area. From 1913-1922, he covered miles of territory with his favorite harness race horse, Fannie. She pulled a buggy that was always full of letters and packages to be delivered. People would often be waiting by their mailbox so they could buy some stamps and chat a few minutes to hear the latest news from town. He would also carry their out-going letters and packages back to the post office for them.

Sometimes, when there was too much mail and packages for my Grandpa Harry to deliver, he would load up another horse and buggy for my grandmother to drive. She loved to help him, but she was very competitive. When Grandma Pearl had the opportunity to share the mail route with him, she would turn the job into a race to see who could get finished first. If it was chilly outside, she would eagerly throw a few bricks on the fire to warm while she got ready to go. Then she would wrap those hot bricks in an old blanket to be placed near her feet during the ride. Finally, she would grab her warm, horsehair, lap blanket and her whip before hurrying outside to the waiting buggy.

In the winter, the snowy roads were never plowed; they were just packed-down tracks. So my grandfather would pull out the sleigh and would harness Big Dan to it. Big Dan was a beautiful sorrel, who was full of pep and energy. When the children saw that big horse and sleigh coming into town with several leather straps of sleigh bells jingling, they all wanted a ride. They squealed with delight sitting in the buggy with the mailman as Big Dan trotted down the road a little way. Then, with rosy cheeks and cheerful hearts, the happy children were delivered back to town.

During those early 1900's, such simple pleasures brought joy, laughter, and unforgettable memories for that generation of children. Memories of my own grandparents and dad, who worked hard to deliver Christmas cheer to others, bring a sweet nostalgic pleasure to my heart.

Decades ago, just a week before Christmas, our family doctor announced a special delivery; it's a girl! After having three boys, my birth was good news that brought great joy to my parents.

As I thought about my birth, God reminded me of a beautiful Christmas song about another special arrival. Over 2,000 years ago, God sent the most 'Special Delivery' ever received by folks waiting, longing for Good News to arrive. It didn't come by mail nor by horse and buggy. No one stood at a mailbox waiting for this unexpected package. Born of Mary, angels announced Jesus' birth to shepherds. "And the angel said unto them, 'Fear not, for behold, I bring to you Good News of great joy that will be for all people.'" Luke 2:10

Jesus was sent from heaven, wrapped as a gift of love. He was bound by God's promise of redemption for all the world. He was filled and sealed by the Holy Spirit to accomplish this work of grace, through which we are saved. The wondrous miracle of Christmas is Jesus Christ, the story of his life, death, and resurrection. May this glorious Good News fill you with hope and joy each Christmas season and every day of your life. It's the most wonderful time of the year, so let's celebrate God's most Special Delivery!

"Joy to the world, the Lord has come!
Let earth, receive her King!"

Reflection: You were created by God and sent into this world as a special delivery to bring the Good News to those still waiting to hear about a Savior. Your deliverance from the bondage of sin positions you to have a testimony that can bring life, hope, and joy to those who desire to receive the gift of salvation through Jesus Christ.

Meditation music: Special Delivery or Joy to the World

Grandma's 1920's whip, blanket & sleigh bells

31.

O Come let us Adore Him

Old-fashioned Christmas pageants have always seemed to 'set the stage' for the true meaning of the season. No matter how the production begins, with countless different scenarios, you can trust that it will have the traditional ending. Growing up in a little country church, the Christmas play was the highlight of the year. Each Sunday school class had its usual role assigned according to their age group. The youngest children would always be the sheep. They were great at crawling, although they tended to wander off from the herd. No little lamb was ever lost for too long!

When I was about six or seven years old, our class was assigned to be the angel choir, and I was given a verse to memorize. I remember thinking about how beautiful I was going to look in my white robe, with my feathery wings and my garland halo. I pictured myself as gloriously glowing. I was going to be a true to life angel, so I quickly learned my line, "Do not be afraid, I bring you good news that will cause great joy for all the people." (Luke 2:10)

Over the next few weeks, rehearsals went well. We memorized our lines, practiced how to move our arms like an angel, and we knew where to stand on the stage. We were confident and ready for the big production. Finally, Christmas Sunday morning came, and I was extremely excited! Some of our moms came to the dressing room to help us put on our angel outfits. My long, dark blonde hair hung in layers of glorious banana curls from sleeping all night in old-fashioned 'rag' curlers. Inwardly, I believed that I was going to be the highlight and star of the show. Surely an angel couldn't look more perfect than my beautiful image in the mirror!

Soon, all the children were being lined up according to the timing of their part in the play. When it was time for the angels to appear to the shepherds, we hurried to get to our places to stand. When I glanced at our spot, I thought, "Why are there boards on saw horses? They weren't there at practice, and they are in the way." As we got nearer to those elevated boards, adults began lifting the angels on top of them. I felt my heart panic with fear, and I began shaking as I was lifted high off the floor. That 3 feet of elevation felt like 30 feet. It was dizzying, and all my boldness and visions of stardom began spinning out of control!

Then the curtain opened. The spotlight was on us and there was complete silence...someone kept poking me and whispering my line. Looking into the blinding bright light, finally, I quaveringly whispered to the shepherds, "Do not be afraid..." I'm pretty sure no one in the audience was convinced that I was sent from God with Good News of great joy. I was the least authentic character in the whole production. Fear and self-preservation stole my confidence. Dreams of grandeur deflated the message I was sent to share.

Looking back, God has allowed me to see the disaster of being 'full of myself.' Wrongly imagining myself as the 'glorious one to be adored' set me up for failure as I attempted to share the Good News of Jesus. When God speaks to my spirit to share His heart of love, mercy and redemption to people around me, my focus has to be Christ-centered. That message must be authentic and full of God's compassion. My own passion must be pure and holy. My humbleness before His throne positions me to receive His words that bring truth and everlasting life to those He sends into my life.

"For we speak as messengers approved by God to be entrusted with the Good News. Our purpose is to please God, not people. He alone examines the motives of our hearts. We loved you so much that we shared with you not only God's Good News but our own lives, too." 1Thessalonians 2:4,8 (NLT)

This Christmas season, let God examine the motives of your heart. He is entrusting you to be His messenger of the Good News. Share your very life with others. Your purpose is to please God by loving people and telling them about Jesus. Salvation came through the lowly birth of His Majesty. Born in the humbleness of a stable, our Savior set the stage for our lives.

Through authentic humility, the role we were assigned to perform in this eternal story of redemption will bring all glory and adoration to God's Son. No angel, St. Nick, or snowman should stand in the spotlight meant only for the Star of this production. Let this Christmas story be a reminder that all of the splendor of heaven shines its light on the Babe of Bethlehem. Born to die, raised in victory, Jesus reigns forever as the King of Kings. Let us rejoice for God is with us! Emanuel has come!

"O come let us adore Him, O come let us adore Him,
O Come let us adore Him, Christ the Lord!"

Reflection: Is there any issue in my heart that prevents me from sharing my testimony of God's grace with others? Has pridefulness or fear of intimidation caused me to remain silent in order to protect myself from embarrassing rejection? Remember, you are a messenger approved by God and you have been entrusted with the Good News...so be fearless!

Meditation music: Breath of Heaven or O Come All Ye Faithful

32

Night of Miracles

Remembering Christmas traditions brings back wonderful memories from my childhood. Every year, my dad would cut down a pine tree in the woods and set it on the porch for a few days until the snow melted. The day before Christmas, our house-full of kids was alive with excitement. Cleverly, our mom would set the dining room table with gigantic bowls of popcorn, multiple packs of colored construction paper, scissors, shakers of glitter, and a lot of tubs of paste. She would help the little ones thread their needles for jabbing the popcorn, then she would disappear for a while into her bedroom. I always assumed an elf was helping her wrap gifts. Meanwhile, we were busy for hours making long strings of popcorn garland and endless feet of construction paper chains. Being egged on by our competitiveness to see who could make the longest strands, we sat there seemingly forever.

Finally, late in the afternoon, my dad would drag the tree inside, and he would wrap it with strings of colored lights. The lights were tested to make sure they worked, then unplugged. After he placed the star on top, we would proudly take a turn putting our home-made decorations on the branches. We thought it looked beautiful. By then, supper would be ready, and afterwards mom would send us to our bedrooms to put on our pajamas. Soon, we were nestled together on the couch and chairs around the TV to watch a few animated Christmas tales like 'Rudolph the Red-Nosed Reindeer' and 'The Night Before Christmas.'

Somehow, every year, like clockwork, just as the last story ended, we would begin to hear the sound of sleigh bells jingling outside. The sound always seemed to be circling our house, and we would run from window to window trying to catch a glimpse of Santa and his sleigh. We'd quickly set out a plate of cookies, then Mom would say, "Hurry and get upstairs to bed. Santa must be in the neighborhood, but he won't stop if you're not sleeping." Little did we know at the time that it was a calculated tactic to hurry us off to bed. That mischievous Santa's helper outside was my fun-loving Aunt Toots, who was sneaking around our house shaking leather straps of sleigh bells, probably from off our grandfather's horses.

I still remember one Christmas clearly, as if it was yesterday. During the middle of the night, I woke up and hoped that Santa didn't pass by our house without stopping. I couldn't stop worrying, so I slipped out of bed, quietly opened my door, then sat down at the top of the stairs. Silently, I slid down one step at a time, until I could see the outline of the tree. As my eyes adjusted to the darkness, I was able to see the shadowy, small stacks of gifts surrounding it. Relieved to know Santa had delivered our presents, I snuck back upstairs to bed and peacefully slept.

When morning dawned, and mama stood at the bottom of the steps calling for us to wake up and come down, I already knew Santa had brought us gifts. Surprisingly, what took my breath away was the miraculous transformation of the tree. It was plugged in and gloriously aglow with colored lights twinkling, glittery ornaments sparkling, silver icicles shimmering, and the golden star on top was shining a magical warmth over the room. I stood mesmerized as the wondrous tree was emblazoned in my memory.

Many decades later, when Christmas Eve has come, I often think about the overnight miraculous transformation of that simple pine tree that my parents elaborately decorated after we went to bed. What a precious gift of love that went beyond our expectations.

In somewhat the same way, our Heavenly Father presented the world with the most spectacular gift of love ever, while many of us were sleeping in darkness. Millions of stars in the heavenlies bowed in awe as the Star of David appeared that night, shining over the birthplace of the Messiah. Isaiah's prophecy, "The people walking in darkness have seen a great light…" was fulfilled. It was a night of miracles, when the tiny baby Jesus, containing all of who God is, was born in a stable in Bethlehem. "The Word became flesh and made his dwelling among us. We have seen his glory, the glory of the one and only Son, who came from the Father, full of grace and truth." John 1:1,14 Jesus became like us, so that we would see His glory manifested through God's plan of salvation.

This story could end now, but it's not yet complete. Yesterday, while I was leading a Bible study at a local nursing-rehab center, the Lord brought to my mind another story to share with the folks. Years ago, after Christmas was over, our new pastor asked for the two Christmas trees that had adorned the front of the church. I assumed he was going to put them in his yard to hang bird food on them. Months later, when Good Friday came and we went to the church service, those same Christmas trees had reappeared in the sanctuary, by the altar. The trees had been stripped of needles, and the branches were broken and cut off. The trees were tied together with ropes to form a cross and were secured by long nails, and then draped in black cloth. The once beautifully adorned trees, which had represented the miracle of Jesus' birth, now had become the old rugged cross, representing his death. They had been transformed like Christ in his suffering, when He was stripped, broken, cut, and secured on a tree by long nails driven into his hands and feet. It was a somber church service.

Sunday morning came and another spectacular scene awaited the congregation. The Christmas tree cross had continued to be transformed. Death was not the end for this pine tree. Now draped in gleaming white and royal purple satin, surrounded by Easter lilies at the foot of the cross, the old Christmas tree vividly stood, proudly proclaiming Jesus' victory over death. Its visual message declared to all, "The King of Kings lives, and His kingdom will reign now and forevermore!"

This Christmas, rejoice in this spectacular gift of love sent from our Heavenly Father. May the thrill of knowing Jesus Christ as your Savior fill you with awe as you behold this divine Night of Miracles.

> "O Holy Night, the stars are brightly shining;
> It is the night of the dear Savior's birth...
> Fall on your knees; O hear the angel voices!
> O night divine, O night when Christ was born.
> O night, O Holy night, O night divine!"

Reflection: Has the night of miracles transformed your life as those Christmas trees which were changed to bear the cross of death, and then become a display of Christ's victory? Have you become one with Christ, sharing in His death and in His resurrection—being raised from sin's death into a victorious life of power and grace?

Meditation music: Christmas Canon or O Holy Night

33.

Life in a Bubble

There are some things in life that seem so simple yet are a source of fascination no matter what our age. Watching clouds float along forming puffy portraits, being mesmerized by the flames of a campfire, and endlessly blowing bubbles not only draws the attention of children but also grownups. Most adults would be embarrassed to admit to blowing bubbles. We may not buy them for ourselves, but often when kids are playing with them, we experience a driving urge to show them the true capabilities of that wand and soapy liquid. I have found myself blowing big impressive bubbles while tuning out those little voices asking for another turn. Even when I gave the wand back to them, I stayed, watched, and marveled at the rainbow swirls that surrounded those tiny circles as they drifted in the breeze.

Pardon my daydreaming, but this morning has been difficult. It has been as appealing as the cooked horsefly floating in my coffee that I just reheated in the microwave. Struggling with some issues in my life has caused such a distraction, that during my quiet time with God, I felt as if no one showed up but me. Trying to break through to God, I repented for any ungodly attitudes in my situation and pleaded for Him to show me His direction in the matter. Remaining in prayer for a while didn't bring the answers that I wanted or hoped would come. I felt that God had left me in a state of limbo. When those frustrating moments come, and they have come for all of us, we want them to be resolved "yesterday," so to speak. After all, Christians shouldn't have to endure long periods of stressful discomfort while waiting. Through Christ, I should have a direct line to the throne room, but why didn't God pick up the ringing phone this morning? I just don't get it...or do I?

My first instinct to find solace after God's silent treatment was to email a close friend and spill the beans—pour out my problems. Truly, God has given me compassionate, caring friends who would have been wonderful at consoling me today. But as I sat typing a message earlier, I couldn't finish the last few words to send it. I knew that I was to continue to lay my burden before my Father, not someone else. I realized that the word of comfort and direction had already been written centuries ago for this heart wrenching moment of mine. 1 Peter 5:6-9 tells us to "Humble yourselves, therefore, under God's mighty hand that he may lift you up in due time. Cast all your anxiety on him because he cares for you. Be self-controlled and alert. Your enemy the devil prowls around like a roaring lion looking for someone to devour. Resist him, standing firm in the faith, because you know that your brothers throughout the world are undergoing the same kind of sufferings."

God's Word says to humble ourselves, and in due time—not our time, He will lift us up. His hand is below lifting us, but we are also "under God's mighty hand." His hands surround and encircle us like a protective bubble. It's like the true story of the boy who lived his life in a bubble. He had no immune system and couldn't tolerate germs. A huge, germ-free, plastic bubble was made for him to live inside in order to prolong his life. Going outside the bubble meant sure death. Germs able to penetrate the shell would have been life threatening to him, and a battle to survive would have needed to be fought. In a similar way, for us, being outside the bubble of Christ's covering means sure death.

But even within that covering, only a pinhole is needed for bacteria to sneak in, attack, and cause disaster. The occasional struggles and periods of discomfort we have actually keep us alert and fit for the warfare that we face. If God didn't allow those experiences to build our defenses, we could easily be blindsided and devastated by the enemy. Oddly enough, it's those past and present battle scars that make our testimony powerful. The sincerity of exposing our imperfections and moments of vulnerability are the very parallels that people can understand and relate to in their own lives. The war games of Satan are twice defeated as God not only ends the invasion but also binds our wounds—using them as evidence of His love. Seeing the faithfulness of God gives others a glimpse of the hope they too can have in the Father's care.

This morning during God's temporary silent treatment, my first instinct wasn't to keep calling out to Him, as if pressing the redial button on my old-fashioned phone. Instead, I quickly turned to a friend. It doesn't matter that God stopped me; my intention was sadly clear. When I felt distant from God, I needed to keep searching after Him. Opening the Bible would have been the wisest choice, but God can be found in *all* that He created. He has ordained everything for His purposes. Even in my earlier diversion to my childhood fascination of clouds, flames, and bubble, He was there. The portraits in the clouds remind me of God expressing His love and pleasure toward us, as He amuses us with puffy images in the heavens. Flames of fire signify the work of the Holy Spirit in cleansing, refining, and empowering our lives. Two thousand years ago, God picked up the wand, blew His breath, and sent His Son through the circle of time and space. Jesus, who died on the cross for our sins, made it possible for His translucent bubble to surround us. Best of all, within that protective bubble of salvation, we are promised eternal life with Him. "And the God of all grace, who called you to his eternal glory in Christ, after you have suffered a little while, will himself restore you and make you strong, firm, and steadfast. To him be the power for ever and ever. Amen." 1 Peter 5:10-11.

LET'S TALK ~ GOD'S HEART FOR YOU

Hello...hello...hello, God, are you there? There's a world-wide pandemic going on, along with rioting mobs, shooting in the streets, and political unrest...would you please answer the phone soon?

Sometimes it feels as if God is not listening. It seems like He must not care. People are in a panic. It's like the lid was lifted off of Pandora's box and no one can close and lock it again in this endless time of trouble and unrest. It's only mid-summer in the year of 2020, and it seems that the craziness is escalating. If the Lord doesn't hear our prayers ringing out as a call for help, who knows if we will survive this mess!

Many folks, young and old, are living in a state of fear, with their minds questioning the future and worrying about an array of "what ifs." If that is how you are feeling, you are not alone! Do you know that the Bible says that fear is not of God? 2 Timothy 1:7 (NKJV) tells us, "God has not given us a spirit of fear, but of power and of love, and of a sound mind." Fear is actually a tactic of the evil one to disable and stun you to prevent you from living a full, unintimidated lifestyle.

First of all, Isaiah 41:10 says, "So do not fear, for I am with you; do not be dismayed, for I am your God. I will strengthen you and help you; I will uphold you with my righteous right hand." God promises to strengthen and help you. Picture God's right hand protecting and holding you up. Isaiah 49:16 (NLT) declares, "I have written your name on the palms of my hand." Now envision that you are watching the Lord engrave your name on His powerful hand. Isaiah 51:16 tells us, "I have put my words in your mouth and covered you with the shadow of My hand..." Last, imagine that you see the Lord lifting His left hand so that you are hidden under its shadow. Each day, set aside time to meditate on these passages so that you can fortify and change the pathway of your thoughts. Your fears will be released as you continually visualize God's loving care.

Isn't it clear that those verses are describing the protective covering of God's hands all around you? If you are one of God's children, then you can trust that this is His promise of security. His hand surrounds you like a bubble of bullet proof glass. It's within this sphere that you will find His Presence prevailing. It is where you can become in sync with the heartbeat of God. It is where you are able to become one with Christ Jesus, acquiring His passion and anointing to minister to the lives of others.

In turbulent times, there is nothing more important than to be able to sense what is going on in the spiritual realm. We need to be able to discern the deception we see playing out on the physical, public stage where people are being manipulated like puppets from overhead strings. Many are being cued lines of a twisted narrative intended to brainwash an audience. It reminds me of the verse in Ephesians 6:12 "For our struggle is not against flesh and blood, but against the rulers, against the authorities, against the powers of this dark world and against the spiritual forces of evil in the heavenly realms." Our struggle is not against those being used as actors, but it is against the puppet masters which are the unseen spiritual forces of evil, straight from the realm of hell.

Therefore, it is imperative that we seek God and allow Him to develop His heavenly perspective within us, so we can understand the battle that is going on right now. We are not to allow ourselves to be caught up in the hatred of misguided people. Our battle is not against them but against the enemy, who is the driving force which is manipulating them. Always remember that love is of God. We can hate what people do, but we are to love them like Jesus does. We are to pray for their salvation. Can you imagine how miserable and wretched they must feel inside? They need Jesus!

More and more, I think that God will be putting us into situations where we are to touch the lives of people around us. I know that the Lord wants to use us in a mighty way, therefore, we need to be trained by the Holy Spirit to walk in the power and authority we have been given through Jesus Christ. We will be like ministering angels to those who are suffering with fear, pain, and hopelessness. Today, I came across a poem written by a dear friend of mine a few years ago. It's a marvelous example of the Lord's compassion flowing through her heart as she went through an unexpected, unwanted situation.

Why Was I There?
By Beverly Saeler Charpentier

Why was I there?
In a room, two mothers alone
The only sound, pain-filled moans.
Separated only by a hospital curtain,
I wasn't completely certain.

Why was I there?
Each was the mother of nine.
She loved her children and I love mine.
We had been together a few short hours,
Brought to this room by a higher power.

Why was I there?
She was confused and unable to speak.
Fighting her illness had left her tired and weak.
In the darkened room I began to pray.
I asked the Angels to come and take her away.

Why was I there?
The room filled with her loved ones only hours before,
Caring nurses, in and out of the door.
As we lay separate, yet together, I felt a bond.
We reached out for help from beyond.

Why was I there?
I not only prayed, I sang songs softy too.
Amazing Grace and The Old Rugged Cross rang true.
I was moved to sing her a lullaby under my breath.
I prayed for her soul and a peaceful death.

Why was I there?
Be calm little Mother, be still little Mother.
The Father says be calm, be still little Mother.
As I sang, the room became very quiet.
There was silence, I couldn't deny it.

Why was I there?
Soon it was confirmed, she had passed.
She was at peace now, with her Father at last.
I see now it was always His plan,
For me to be there when she took His hand.

Why was I there?
God put me there!

What a powerful testimony Beverly shared about her experience. It wasn't one that she would have chosen for herself but God needed her there. Only God knows why He has placed you in this time and season. Seek after God. He will be found if you seek Him with all your heart, mind, and soul. There is a power-filled life that God wants to prepare you to walk in. There will be places that God will send you that you may later wonder and ask, "Why was I there?" You might not know the answer to the 'why' but you will trust God and know that He put you there for a purpose. You were created to carry out His special assignments. It may be in a hospital room, a grocery store, on a sidewalk, or any random place where God has set up a divine appointment that only you may have an opportunity to reach someone with His love. You may speak a kind word of hope, share a smile, or pray for healing.

This may not be the summer for gazing at clouds, campfires or blowing bubbles, but we may behold something more awesome—the glory of God. Behind the stage curtain, behind the chaos, have no doubt that God is ultimately running the control panel. His hands have access to all the lighting, audio sliders, switches, and power cords. With that in mind, in His perfect timing, expect to see the unfolding of God's final act taking the limelight as His righteousness is released, revelation is revealed, repentance is rendered, and revival is regenerated throughout this land that was established as His covenant nation. Pray for the Holy Spirit to come like tongues of fire and begin preparing hearts for the great harvest of souls. May this be the beginning of the great awakening when millions will be brought into the kingdom of God. The time is drawing closer to when people of every nation and all of creation shall bow before the Ancient of Days. Every tongue in heaven and earth will declare His glory. The spectacular finale of this closing performance will be glorious!

Reflection: Father God, keep me aware that I am surrounded by Your hands so that fear will have no place in my spirit. Synchronize my heart with Yours, Lord, that I may share my testimony and bring others to know you as Savior. Amen.

Meditation music: Ancient of Days or We've a Story to Tell to the Nations

34.

The
Most Incredible Journey

How did this story begin; how will this epic journey end? After a moment of thought, the most obvious answer came to me... God, the Alpha and the Omega, the Beginning and the End. He had already mapped it out for me to follow.

Years ago, God challenged me to journal my way through the entire Bible. He instructed me to read each section or chapter, along with all the study notes, and then allow the Holy Spirit to guide my thoughts as I wrote down the things that He wanted me to understand. It was the most life-awakening, life-enlightening, life-transforming journey that I have ever experienced. The intense, sensational trip with my Father took two and a half years to travel from Genesis through Revelation.

As I look back, God had been preparing me in advance for this trip of a lifetime. He had me packing my bag with everything that I would need for an extended journey on a scenic train tour, pre-planned with sixty-six stops that would be filled with adventurous excursions. Along the way, I figured that we would encounter a few detours and delays, but I felt confident that the train would eventually keep us moving forward, toward the final destination and my destiny.

One important preparation began when God put me into a Bible study that was called Communion with God. Through it, the Lord taught me how to quiet my soul so that I could receive a better understanding of who He is. "Be still and know that I Am God..." Psalm 41:10. It was instrumental in teaching me to listen for His Voice, while waiting for the fullness of His Presence to come. Experiencing God's closeness gave me courage to ask Him about difficult times in my past, so that my wounded heart could begin to heal. He lovingly gave me vision to see where He was during many circumstances throughout my life. Even if I felt alone during times of crisis, I know that He never left my side. My Father revealed things to me that were important to be aware of for the journey ahead. At that same time, God was teaching me obedience. Learning to obey without hesitation would require me to push through monstrous fears at times and heart-wrenching tears. The practice of absolute submission was necessary to trigger a spontaneous response to trust God unconditionally, especially at times when I was sent off to explore the unknown.

Another interesting thing that happened about that same time was the Lord began to tell me that He was going to lead me into the 'wilderness.' He would pop that word into my thoughts while I was listening to a song called 'Beautiful River,' and while I was praying. The first time it happened, I remember thinking that God must be warning me of a coming season in my life that would be like forty years of wandering in the stifling desert. Graciously, He didn't let me fret too long before letting me know that it would be more like an adventure into the wilderness of a lush, new land, filled with spectacular sights to behold. We'd be together like the early pioneers, riding along on the front seat of a Conestoga wagon with Him holding the reins of a powerful team of horses. My place was to just sit close like a new bride, with an open Bible on my lap like a loaded shotgun ready to aim at any predators. The full weight of the Word would keep me anchored like a rock in my seat, as the ride dipped into valleys and climbed steep slopes. What an adventurous trip it would be!

During the first month of this new journey, we boarded the passenger train to travel through Genesis. It was fascinating to imagine what it looked like as God spoke and formed the world and all living creatures. It was amazing to be reminded that we are made in God's image like Adam and Eve. God breathed life into each of us. What awesome stories of unforgettable characters we encountered throughout the history of mankind. When we arrived at chapter 22, I read a story of profound faith and obedience. God spoke to Abraham and said, "Take your son, your only son, whom you love—Isaac—and go to the region of Moriah. Sacrifice him there as a burnt offering on a mountain I will show you." Abraham obeyed by offering his son as a holy sacrifice on an altar. Before he could kill Isaac, the angel of the Lord stopped him and said, "Do not do anything to him. Now I know that you fear God, because you have not withheld from me your son, your only son." At that moment, God nudged my heart to offer Him a holy sacrifice. I wasn't as brave as Abraham to do exactly what he did. Instead, I thought about the things that I loved most in my life. In all sincerity, I placed on the altar my love of reading books, my love of teaching piano, my love of camping, and my love of being part of the praise team. Through many heartfelt tears, I surrendered them one by one, expecting God to receive them at that very moment as my sacrifice. But He sent no flame to consume them and allowed my offering to remain there—at least for a time.

Before we left Genesis, the book of God's wondrous story of creation, He brought to my life a new birth. I was unaware that I was even expecting. But one night, about a week after offering my sacrifice to God, I had gone to bed following a mild disagreement with my husband. I couldn't sleep because, like most women tend to do, in my mind, I kept rehashing our conversation. Finally, I got out of bed and went to the living room, where I picked up my Bible and journal; then I began to read and pray. Suddenly, God gave me a vision of a large house. There was a sign in the front yard that said Hope House Ministries. Then I heard Him speaking to my heart about some details, so I quickly opened my journal to write them down. The Lord told me that this ministry would teach Bible studies, host retreats, and sponsor outreaches. As I wondered how this would come to be, He reminded me about my prayer group. He had already prepared these trusted friends to support the ministry work ahead. None of this was my idea; it was God's plan to birth a ministry through me. My role in this plan was to trust Him. "Trust in the Lord with all your heart, and lean not on your own understanding; In all your ways acknowledge Him, and He will make your path straight." Proverbs 3:5-6 (BSB) No matter how fearful my introverted spirit felt, acknowledging God to be my Vision, the Lord of my heart, brought peace to my soul that night.

> Be Thou my Vision, O Lord of my heart;
> Naught be all else to me, save that Thou art
> Thou my best Thought, by day or by night,
> Waking or sleeping, Thy presence my light.

When I woke the next day, I was overwhelmed by God's revelation, but I tried to function normally. I couldn't think straight, I couldn't eat, and I couldn't focus on my job. Finally, at the end of the day, I shared the vision of ministry with my husband. Later I shared it with my two mentors, one of whom the Lord gave a prophetic word to speak to me. It was from Revelation 3:8. "I know your deeds. See, I have placed before you an open door that no one can shut. I know that you have little strength, yet you kept my word and have not denied my name." It was a word from the Lord that kept me strong throughout the building of the ministry and especially as we endured years of persecution. No man has been able to shut God's open door.

Meanwhile, we prayed for God to unfold His plan, and a few months later we shared it with the rest of our group. It remained dedicated to prayer for over a year before actual ministry began. Although the ministry was not active outside of our group during that time, inside God was training us to know how to minister to others. He filled us with compassion to love deeply and vision to really see people—looking beyond the physical to the spiritual needs of healing the heart and soul. It was a time for God to build our confidence to trust Him when the Holy Spirit nudged us to move on His behalf. Without the Lord's training, our faith could have wavered in the future, when the enemy would attempt to block the leading of God's Spirit.

Soon we boarded the train to get some rest until it was time to exit into Exodus. What a refreshing land of freedom! God broke chains of intimidation and fear that had kept me bound by the enemy for years, to keep me in a place where my testimony was confined. I was enslaved by extreme shyness which locked me into a prison of self-protection. But God opened the door and set me free to fulfill His calling on my life. Not only did the Lord grant me spiritual freedom, but He gave me freedom from worrying about how Hope House Ministry would be financed. I remember being very concerned about the enormous cost to build this vision into reality.

God showed me the answer in chapter 35:4-5, 20-21. When Moses was ready to build the tabernacle, he assembled the whole Israelite community and said to them, "This is what the Lord has commanded: From what you have, take an offering for the Lord. *Everyone who is willing* is to bring to the Lord an offering...Then the whole Israelite community withdrew from Moses' presence, and *everyone who was willing and whose heart moved them* came and brought an offering to the Lord for the work on the tent of meeting, for all its service, and for the sacred garments." The key phrases were emphasized twice. The Lord was showing me that the finances needed would come as offerings from *everyone who was willing and whose heart He would move* to support the ministry. It wasn't going to be my job to convince people to give; it was the Holy Spirit who would be responsible to move people's hearts.

At that same time, the Lord put a word of His promised provision on the heart of a stranger who shared it with us. We were told that Hope House would have a tree in its yard that would ripen fruit, just as it was needed. Not only did the Lord give us Scripture about the income needed, but He confirmed it through someone who actually lived in a different city and knew nothing about us. Since that time, God moved the heart of my step-father, Robert Heichel, to donate our family home and property to the ministry. And God also touched the hearts of my five brothers (Harry, Larry, Stanley, Douglas, and Brian) and two sisters (Christine and Rebecca) to readily agree to the decision, which eliminated their inheritance. Over the years, the Lord has continually financed Hope House through willing people. We have received the funds needed for maintenance work, updating the building, and supplies for all the Bible studies and outreaches that we have sponsored. God, our Tree of Provision, has been faithful.

Slowly chugging through the land of Leviticus, which was tediously full of detailed guidelines, laws and regulations for the health and welfare of the Jewish nation, the Lord gave me the startling realization that He had very detailed guidelines for our ministry. His mandate would need to be followed just as strictly for its health and welfare. It was imperative that the standards that the Lord set would be carefully worded in our ministry bylaws and followed by everyone involved in leadership roles within Hope House.

Traveling through each book of the Bible has brought new revelation into my personal life and into the life of the ministry that God has been building. When I needed encouraged, the Word would speak to me as real as if my Father was sitting beside me. One day He introduced me to Uncle Ezra, who taught me the importance of living a righteous life that was not corrupted by ungodly influences. After finishing the book, I woke the next morning with my Father telling me that I was not quite through with Ezra yet. He gave me a visual picture of our old family reunions, which were held near a pond on my grandfather's property when I was growing up. The Lord told me to go and setup my lawn chair beside Uncle Ezra, for I still had much to learn from him.

So, I re-read the amazing story of this priest, who had devoted himself to the study and observance of the Law of the Lord, which he taught to the Israelites. Therefore, God chose him to lead a large group out of captivity from Babylon back to their homeland. God gave Ezra great favor with the King who released them, along with great wealth, to rebuild their homes and the city of Jerusalem. One unforgettable moment in the story came when Ezra was made aware of the sinfulness of the exiles, who had broken God's law and had intermarried with pagans. When Ezra heard, he tore his clothes, pulled out his hair, and mourned. Chapter 10:1 says, "While Ezra was praying and confessing, weeping and throwing himself down before the house of God, a large crowd of Israelites—men, women and children—gathered around him..." Although Ezra carried no guilt of his own, he repented in behalf of those who were guilty. When they saw Ezra's devastation, they all fell weeping in repentance. Through this story, the Lord was showing me the powerful effectiveness of a person who was devoted to God and lived a life in a manner that was pleasing to Him. It was a lesson on integrity and righteousness that was imperative to understand. It was well-worth the train delay.

Eventually, we traveled through Persia to the palace of King Xerxes to visit Great Grandma Esther. What a story she had to share! She reminded me that even when the odds seem to be against whatever you need to do, you can trust the Lord to pull off an amazing, triumph-filled victory. God sometimes puts us in dire situations in which He is the only one who has the answer that can solve the problem. Without His intervention, we would surely be doomed. But God can outwit every scheme of the enemy. Because of Esther's faith, the whole Jewish nation was saved from death. Being inspired by the queen's testimony, I know that I can face anything because God is with me. In Esther 4:14, we find the infamous verse which ends with these words, "And who knows but that you have come to your royal position for such a time as this?" I can't say that I feel like I'm in a royal position, but I do know that I am alive "for such a time as this" to fulfill the destiny that God planned for me. It is the exact time in history that God sent you and me to be born to live out our lives. It is our moment of truth to face death-defying odds in order that God's glory would be revealed in an undeniable way.

Settling into the train's sleeper car after the exhilarating, yet exhausting, visit at the castle, I have found my hiding place in the book of Psalms: I am hidden in the cleft of the Rock, covered by the shadow of His Hand. The Lord is my Shepherd and my Comforter; I rest in the Arms of my Father. Through good times and hard times, He has been my strong tower and strength. He has kept me safely enclosed within His fortress walls, and I have been blessed by His loving care. He formed me, knows me, and keeps me under His watchful eye every moment of the day. I am never alone for He is with me wherever I am.

Traveling along through the Holy Land, my encounter with Isaiah brought a prophetic voice of hope into my life. It has encouraged me when I have needed a boost of spiritual energy to keep moving. This book calls us to repentance, then promises us redemption through God's mercy and forgiveness. His unfailing love becomes the bridge that leads us to restoration, so that our lives can be rebuilt. "He will be the sure foundation for your times, a rich store of salvation and wisdom and knowledge; the fear of the Lord is the key to this treasure." Isaiah 33:6. God has to be our firm foundation. In Him, we are given access to a rich storehouse of salvation, wisdom and knowledge, which prepares us in advance for whatever God directs us to do.

This morning, there was a melody stirring in my soul as I woke, and I knew that I was to come sit in God's presence. For the past few months, God has been wooing my heart with those song lyrics to bring me to our quiet place to finish the work that needs done. Sometimes I avoid doing it because I feel a sense of unworthiness to share God's Heart with others. What if I mess up and disappoint Him? I know that I am not enough without Him. But, if He meets with me, I know that we can do this together. Isaiah said that the fear of the Lord is the key to this storehouse of treasure. Our sense of God's Majesty must be so intense that we are completely humbled in His Presence. When our hearts are surrendered unto submission, it lifts the lid of the treasure chest for us to see our Father's Heart.

After years of traveling and touring sixty-five books along the way, the most incredible journey was slowly coming to an end. Before studying the final Word of the Lord, I found a comfy chair in the parlor car as I rode the train through John's vision of Revelation. Observing it at a safe distance was one of my better ideas that I've had on this trip. Honestly, sometimes I found myself trying to hide my face behind the drapes hanging on the window. Some of the scenes reminded me of watching a scary sci-fi movie. I wanted to watch but had to look away at times. It seemed unbelievable, yet I knew this was real. My mind was being overwhelmingly stimulated by God's vivid proclamation of what His justice and final victory will look like. If I had experienced no other book, this one would have brought me to my knees out of guilt and fear. My fear of the wrath of God would have driven me to surrender myself for salvation. Although we deserve His wrath, it was God's great love for us that over-rode our demise. It was His unfathomable love and grace that draws our hearts to receive the gift that was paid for by Jesus Christ. God's plan made Satan wildly furious. It has driven him to falsely accuse us day and night before God, in an attempt to destroy our future and eternal life. Yet it is clearly written in the book that Christ Jesus has already been declared victorious! He has been robed in majesty and crowned the King of Kings.

John wrote in Revelation 21:6, "He said to me: It is done. I am the Alpha and the Omega, the Beginning and the End. To the thirsty I will give water without cost from the spring of the water of life." When I came to this verse, I felt as if God was telling me that my job of writing this book was done. Through His inspiration, we have offered anyone who is thirsty, water from the living springs–Jesus. My story began with the Lord nudging my heart to come with Him on the trip of a lifetime. I pray that my epic journey will end with God nudging your heart to pack your bags for your own sensational time with Him. I promise that you will never regret the sacrifice that it may require. Get on board with the Lord; together you will experience the most incredible journey ever!

LET'S TALK ~ GOD'S HEART FOR YOU

If I were to write down everything that God has taught me on our journey together, it would fill volumes. Many stories in this book were written while I was on the journey. The remainder came over the years, as God would plant story ideas in my head, along with verses that seemed to fit perfectly. As for my mention earlier in the story about the sacrifices that I laid on the altar and offered to the Lord, He eventually accepted every one of them. I have no regrets about losing those 'loves' because, in their place, God grew my love for Himself.

God's heart for you is that you would grow to love Him deeper and experience the completeness that is found in His all-encompassing love for you. Open your heart to be taught by your Father, and allow Him to take you on a magnificent journey. He has already mapped out the route that will bring you into the destiny that you were created to fulfill at this precise moment in history. Trust me, it will be an awesome ride when you are on-track with the Lord. So, get packing!

Working on this last story over the weekend, I found myself thinking, "Well, I guess this is it for me. My destiny work is done; I am finally completing this book." Imagine my surprise when a couple of ladies at church, who didn't know I was writing a book, walked over to me during prayer time and wanted to pray for me. They felt the Lord wanted to tell me that God wasn't through with me yet. They told me that I was not done but would be continuing on in my work with Him.

Well, I'm not sure what that means. But after a time of rest, I pray that the Holy Spirit will stir up a restlessness in my soul and I will long for another amazing adventure. I was reminded of a chat I had with my dear friend when we were text-talking about the artwork for this book and the ideas for another project that's been in the back of our minds. We were so excited about how God was bringing it all together, and we were text-giggling about how much fun we were having. Then I said to her, "We're like little hobo girls on a run-away train, feet dangling and hair blowing in the wind, and a song on our lips...

'This is my story, this is my song; Praising my Savior, all the day long.

This is my story, this is my song; Praising my Savior, all the day long.'"

AMEN and AMEN!

Editor Ann ~ Writer Sue ~ Artist Georgene

MESSAGE FROM THE AUTHOR

In my office, there is a wall lined with glass enclosed bookshelves. I have always loved my books, and I wanted to protect them from a dust bunny invasion. But lately I have been thinking, "Why have I kept hundreds of books to myself? I haven't opened them for years." You are probably like me; I normally read a book once, and then I shelve it forever. Maybe it's time to change that pattern. If this book has brought a smile and encouragement to your heart, consider passing it along to another person that may need some joy and inspiration. I pray that "As Taught By My Father" has blessed your life and has drawn you closer to your heavenly Father.

For more information about Hope House Ministries of Adonai, you can check out our Facebook page. If you would like to comment about this book, you may email me at SueP.Protzman@Gmail.com

Georgene Funk is a longtime, local artist who specializes in illustrations. She and her husband Roy are on the Board of Ministries at Hope House and lead outreach endeavors. They reside in Butler, Pa.

"May the Lord bless you and keep you,
may the Lord cause His face to shine upon you
and be gracious to you;
may the Lord lift up His countenance toward you
and give you peace." Amen.
Numbers 6:24-26 (BSB)

CPSIA information can be obtained
at www.ICGtesting.com
Printed in the USA
LVHW070614261120
672695LV00028BA/539